HOW YOU CAN

BOWL
BETTER
USING SELF-HYPNOSIS

JACK HEISE ★ CONTRIBUTORS ★ DON CARTER ★ BUZZ FAZIO
★ THERM GIBSON ★ MARION LADEWIG ★ JOE NORRIS ★

HOW YOU CAN

BOWL
BETTER
USING SELF-HYPNOSIS

by JACK HEISE

author of

How You Can Play Better Golf
Using Self-Hypnosis

★CONTRIBUTORS★

DON CARTER★BUZZ FAZIO

★ THERM GIBSON ★ MARION LADEWIG ★ JOE NORRIS ★

1979 Edition

Published by
Melvin Powers
WILSHIRE BOOK COMPANY
12015 Sherman Road
No. Hollywood, California 91605
Telephone: (213) 875-1711

Printed by

HAL LEIGHTON PRINTING COMPANY
P.O. Box 3952
North Hollywood, California 91605
Telephone: (213) 983-1105

Library of Congress Catalog Card Number 61-16793
Printed in the United States of America
ISBN 0-87980-071-2

Acknowledgments

To the Brunswick Bowling Corporation for their courtesy, cooperation and permission to reprint diagrams and material from their book, SECRETS OF THE STARS, and for supplying photographs of the members of the Brunswick advisory staff of bowling champions.

To Don Carter, Buzz Fazio, Therm Gibson, Marion Ladewig and Joe Norris for their articles on the mental side of bowling.

TENSION NO. 1 ENEMY

by DON CARTER

Member, Brunswick Advisory Staff of Star Bowlers

Who is your most aggressive opponent?

Tension . . . that's your chief enemy!

Every star bowler . . . every bowler who has ever won a tournament has come to grips with this opponent! A vicious foe, tension can play more havoc with your bowling form than any other single element.

What's the solution?

You!

You must face tension . . . you must defeat tension. No one else can help you! The battle is all yours!

What are your best weapons? Concentration . . . determination . . . relaxation . . . and a strong desire to win. Put these to use, and tension can do nothing else but disappear.

Concentrate on your target . . . and have the relaxed form that allows for full concentration and the smooth delivery that spells CHAMPION BOWLER!

RELAXED DETERMINATION

by BUZZ FAZIO

Member, Brunswick Advisory Staff of Star Bowlers

I've watched too many bowlers whose determination to knock the pins down was less than that of the pins to keep standing.

Before they even delivered the ball, I would have given odds the spare would be missed, or the pocket would not be touched.

Obviously, they lacked the determination to bring in that spare or to place the ball in the 1-3 pocket. They gave up before they started their delivery.

Next time you watch bowling on television or are fortunate enough to be in the gallery watching one of the top bowling tournaments, note the determination in the actions of these champions. They treat every frame as if it meant the difference between winning or losing the match. That's determination . . . that's what often spells the difference between just a bowler and a champion bowler.

RELAX...AND BOWL BETTER!

by THERM GIBSON

Member, Brunswick Advisory Staff of Star Bowlers

I know you'll tell me that to say "relax" is easier than doing it.

That may be true . . . but at the same time, relax you must for complete control of your bowling form . . . your ball delivery . . . and, of course, concentration on your target.

Now, how do you relax?

My formula is to first convince myself that I'm bowling properly.

Secondly, my only reason for bowling is to knock over ten pins with one ball as many times as possible. Thirdly, if I miss all ten on the first ball, then the spare is a *must!*

All through bowling I keep telling myself I can do it . . . I can do it! And soon you too will find out that you can be determined . . . you can concentrate . . . and you can be relaxed as you bring in those strikes and spares.

CONVINCING YOURSELF

by MARION LADEWIG

Member, Brunswick Advisory Staff of Star Bowlers

You underrate yourself more than any other bowler!

You're conservative . . . you don't allow yourself to have the optimistic attitude you should.

The next time you're bowling and you're faced with a situation where your frame can be the determining factor in your team winning, your league winning, or you, yourself, winning the match . . . stop for just one second.

Examine yourself!

What's your attitude?

Have you already accepted the fact you'll miss that spare?

Or do you have the confidence in yourself that says, "This spare is as good as made!"

Only until you can answer the last statement in a positive manner have you convinced yourself. And only after you've convinced yourself will you be on your way to a high, consistent bowling average.

CONCENTRATION

by JOE NORRIS

Member, Brunswick Advisory Staff of Star Bowlers

Without doubt, the single quality that every consistent, high average bowler has is concentration.

From the second he picks up his ball until the moment he delivers it, his only thought is the target. Whether it's the strike ball or a spare ball, his only thought is to hit the target.

This same unrelenting concentration applies to every phase of bowling. Be it the first frame, the last frame or the deciding frame in match play, the same concentration must be applied to your bowling.

Blend concentration into your practice and league play. You'll soon find it becoming a habit and you'll enjoy the high-scoring average that goes with it.

Concentrate on your game the next time you bowl.

BOWLING DELIVERIES

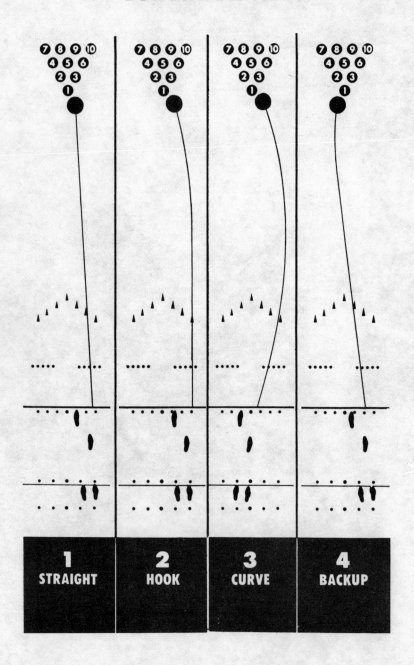

THE STANCE, APPROACH AND FOLLOW-THROUGH

THE 3 STEP APPROACH

To find your starting position pace off 3½ steps from the foul line, do an about face and assume your stance. The first step (1) is with the left foot. Notice that the ball is pushed all the way forward. The ball begins its arc to the rear with the second step (2) and reaches the peak of the backswing. Delivery is made as the last step (3) is made with the left foot. Slide and follow-through complete the delivery. *Best for beginners having difficulty coordinating the 4-step approach.*

THE 4 STEP APPROACH

Pace off 4½ steps from foul line to locate spot for stance. The first step (1) is with the right foot. Pushaway of ball is begun simultaneously with foot movement. Second step (2) finds ball in backswing. Lowest point of swing should be reached as your left heel touches the floor. Third step (3) finds peak of shoulder high backswing reached. Final step (4) finds ball in delivery stage, weight on left foot, right foot providing balance. *Most popular approach. Now recommended for most beginners and regulars alike.*

THE 5 STEP APPROACH

Pace off 5 steps from foul line to locate spot for stance. The first step (1) is short. No pushout is made until the step is completed. The second step (2) is full length with the backswing initiated. The ball is at its lowest point when the weight is on the right foot. As the left heel touches the floor (3) the ball nears its maximum backswing. Step number four (4) finds the ball ready at peak of backswing for delivery and the left foot ready for the final step-slide. With weight on the left foot (5) the ball is delivered.

The 5-step requires slightly more coordination than 4-step. Should be tried to determine which is most natural delivery for individual.

THE FOLLOW THROUGH

Your delivery is not completed with the release of the ball. Your final action is the follow-through, the importance of which cannot be overemphasized since it is so often neglected. Good follow-through is nothing more than the rhythmical completion of your pendulum-like arm swing as it delivers the ball. Your arm should naturally follow the path of the ball until it has reached a natural peak. It should not be to the right or left. It should not be abruptly curtailed. Arm motion to the left, or an arm jerked to a halt will kill the action of the ball since the movement had to be dictated to the muscles prior to the release of the ball. Note too, that the head and eyes are not lifted to follow the course of the ball, but remain on the original target or aiming spot.

PICKING UP SPARES...THE KEY TO SUCCESS
Use your strike ball for these spares.

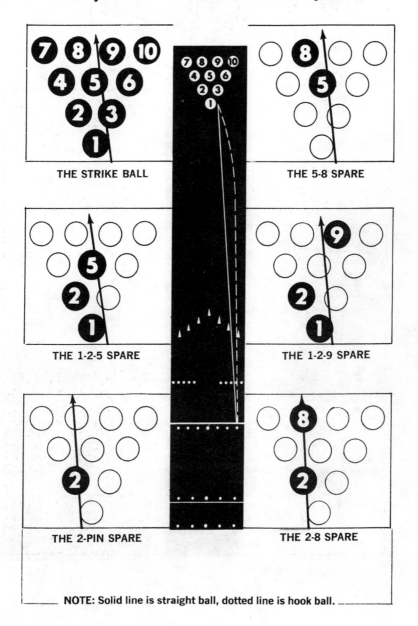

THE STRIKE BALL

THE 5-8 SPARE

THE 1-2-5 SPARE

THE 1-2-9 SPARE

THE 2-PIN SPARE

THE 2-8 SPARE

NOTE: Solid line is straight ball, dotted line is hook ball.

GETTING LEFT-SIDE SPARES

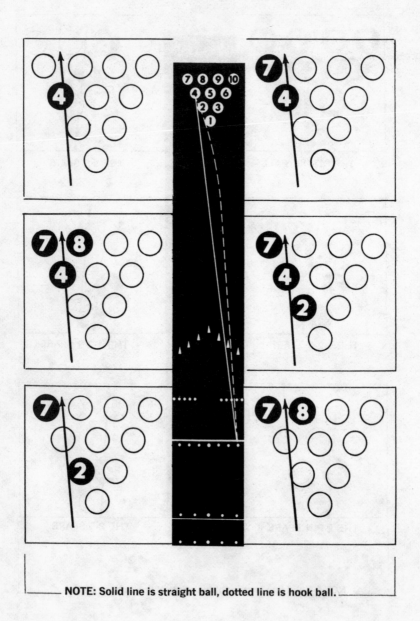

NOTE: Solid line is straight ball, dotted line is hook ball.

CONVERTING RIGHT-HAND SPARES

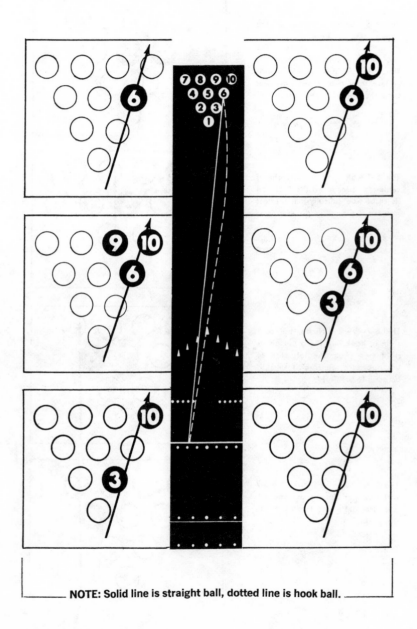

NOTE: Solid line is straight ball, dotted line is hook ball.

CONVERTING THE SPLITS

The 4-5 — Select a target to the right-center of the lane in order to connect squarely between the two pins. Accuracy is essential since the distance between pins is less than two inches narrower than the width of the ball.

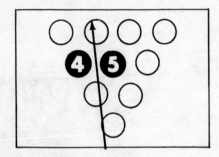

The 5-7 — Start from just right of center in order to hit the 5-pin on its right side causing it to deflect into the 7-pin.

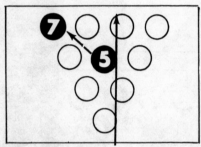

The 6-7 — Very difficult, but possible to hook into the 6-pin on its right side (from the left side of the approach) causing it to skid across into the 7-pin.

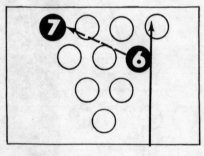

The 6-7-10 — Same shot as the 6-7 with the ball taking out the 10-pin after deflecting the 6-pin into the 7-pin.

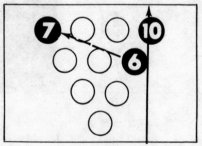

CONVERTING THE SPLITS

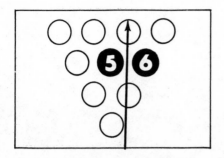

The 5-6—Shoot from left of center in order to connect squarely between the two pins. Accuracy is essential since the distance between pins is less than two inches narrower than the width of the ball.

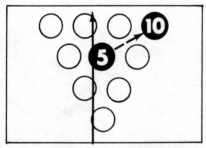

The 5-10—Roll from right-center of lane striking the 5-pin on its left side causing deflection into the 10-pin.

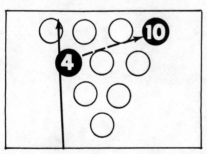

The 4-10—One of the most difficult. From the right side aim to graze the 4-pin on its left side causing it to deflect into the 10-pin.

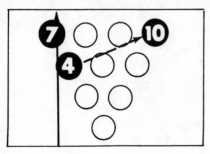

The 4-7-10—Same shot as the 4-10 with the ball taking out the 7-pin after deflecting the 4-pin into the 10-pin.

CONTENTS

Chapter 1

Here's A Promise For Better Bowling

I'VE GOT IT!

Have you ever rolled a perfect strike during a practice session and said to yourself, "I've got it!"?

Even before you released the ball, you knew it was going to be a smash hit in the 1-3 pocket for a clean splash. You had the feeling that everything was just right. Your delivery was like a well-oiled machine and suddenly you understood what the instructors were talking about when they stressed coordination and timing.

Maybe you rolled a double or a turkey and the taps and splits began to fall for spares. It seemed so easy, it was hard to believe you could deliver the ball with such ease and control with so little effort. You knew you had discovered the secret of the Classic league players and the tournament stars.

You may not have marked in every frame, but you knew with a little more practice it wouldn't be long before your average would begin to climb.

Later, you may have tried to analyze what it was that gave you the form and control. You swung an imaginary ball around home to recapture and keep the feeling of that smooth, flowing delivery.

You could hardly wait for the night of your league game. You'd show them how to rack up a score. When your league night came, you stepped confidently up to the approach. And then what happened? Nothing worked. Your confidence evaporated and your game went to pieces again.

And then you began to ponder about that feeling you had during practice. It was like pursuing a will o' the wisp. No amount of imagination could summon up that same unconquerable feeling.

USE YOUR PRACTICE GAME IN LEAGUE PLAY

Keeping that important feeling is what you are going to learn from using self-hypnosis. It is the secret of the champions and high average bowlers who have discovered the means of taking their practice games into tournament and league play.

It is known as the "subconscious feel." Once you have learned how to activate this subconscious feeling and to bowl with the timing, relaxation and coordination possible in practice while under the tension of competition, most of your problems will be solved and you'll be well on the way to the high average you are capable of carrying.

You may be surprised to learn that the top notch bowlers practice often, not to keep physically fit, but to keep in shape mentally. Tournament bowlers get ample exercise in their matches, exhibitions and clinics to keep their muscles in tune.

It is the mental side of bowling that requires constant checking. And most bowling stars put in from 50 to 60 practice games a week in addition to their regular appearances.

THE MENTAL GAME IS TOUGH

Take it from Enrico (Hank) Marino, undefeated world champion, named Bowler of the Half-Century and a member of the Bowling Hall of Fame. Hank says, "It isn't until a bowler enters a tournament or competition, no matter how small it may be, that the mental side of the game asserts itself.

"The one thing that impresses is the incredible change of temperament. This change of mental attitude almost makes a bowler a stranger to himself."

This mental part of the game is just as tough on the stars who have become accustomed to the glare of the television camera lights as it is for the novice bowling his first league game. The only difference is that the champions have learned to control it.

Marino adds, "You've heard it said about certain bowlers that they are without nerves and are as cool as cucumbers. Well, in all the years I've been bowling, I've never met one. There's never been a time when I didn't feel a quickening of the heartbeat and extra nerve pulsations before a match. It's only after it is under way that the calm settles."

You may wonder what there could be about rolling a 16-pound ball down a 60-foot maple lane that should cause undue mental stress.

The great bowling master, Joe Falcaro, explains it as,

"The kegler who feels he has a 300 game in the offing after two or three successive strikes will discover that every delivery gets tougher. His relaxation turns to tension and his muscles tighten. The ball seems to get heavier and more difficult to release. That's the mental side of bowling."

What can you do about it?

THE EXPLANATION IS SIMPLE

The explanation is amazingly simple. All you must be able to do is relax muscle tension. It is the key to co-ordination and timing.

The "Bowling Schoolmaster," Frank Clause, a member of the American Machine and Foundry Company advisory staff (AMF), who won $26,000 in a single night on the television show, "Jackpot Bowling," explains:

"If you start with a working knowledge of the fundamentals of bowling and concentrate on making your body relax as you apply them, you should be able to develop your game to the limits of your ability."

Every star writing on bowling or lecturing at clinics stresses that form is a highly individual matter. The only thing that really counts is being able to relax tension for a smooth delivery.

Carmen Salvino, who started bowling at 12, was in a Classic league at 17 and at 19 was the youngest American Bowling Congress (ABC) titlist, states: "I practice until the game becomes automatic. I don't have to think about what I intend to do with the ball, so I can be completely relaxed and natural when I am in competition."

You could go right through the Bowling Hall of Fame and get identical advice from each of the greats. Ed

Lubanski, Bowler of the Year in 1959, says, "Think what you are going to do as you take your stance. Then, don't think about anything in particular and just learn to spill the pins."

Only the phrasing changes as each of the champions gives advice. Buzz Fazio states it as, "Timing can make or break a bowler. The path to the foul line is short but is strewn with pitfalls if your timing is off. Avoid stiffening. Be calm, relaxed and don't hurry your delivery."

HERE'S THE PROMISE

"Good," you say, "but what happens when I get up to the approach area in competition with my teammates expecting me to come through with a halfway decent score? I feel like a wooden Indian struggling with a cannon ball. The feeling I had during practice is gone and no matter how hard I try, there's no way to recapture it."

You aren't alone in this feeling. There are times when it catches up with the big names, too. You've watched a star carrying a better-than-200 average going for a spare on a televised match dump one in the gutter. You shake your head and say, "How can a guy like that miss?"

The noted television commentator, Fred Wolf, asked the same question of Billy Golembiewski after Billy "G" rolled one that missed a single 5-pin by a good six inches. "Got a little careless on that one, huh Billy?" Wolf chided.

Billy, who has earned a great deal of money from his television performances, including a sports car for a 300-game before the cameras, shook his head. He answered seriously, "I got too careful."

What Billy was saying, and Wolf, a former Stroh's team member appreciated it, was that instead of rolling the ball with his normal, relaxed delivery, he tightened to be sure of toppling the pin and missed it completely.

Detroit's Al Fifer came into the 1944 ABC tournament carrying a healthy average and set an all-time record by rolling eight gutter balls.

You've seen what happens to the stars when they get on "Jackpot Bowling." The players have dubbed it a version of Russian roulette because of the nerve wracking tension. To get an invitation to appear, a kegler must have an average around the 200 mark. Yet many fail to pick up more than two or three strikes and weeks go by before they can stack up six in a row.

During a practice session ahead of this tournament, Harry Smith chalked up 56 strikes out of 60 rolls. Before the cameras he lost to Frank Clause 6 to 5.

"But I'm not under that kind of strain," you say. "I bowl with a bunch of fellows and we're all friends. All I want to do is hold up my end for the team. It's not a life-or-death matter to me to carry a high average. I make my living at another job and bowling is only recreation."

Are you being absolutely truthful with yourself? If you now hold a 120 average, wouldn't you be better satisfied with a 140? Or if you have climbed to 170 or 190, aren't you thinking of that magic 200 figure?

Bowling, like any other competitive sport, holds its fascination because an individual feels he can improve. Like gambling, it holds the glittering promise, "Next time, things will be different."

After consideration, you may agree you'd like to make the Classic league. Maybe even enter some of the big tournaments. And you wouldn't turn down a bid for some of that easy television money. "But how is hypnosis going to help?" you ask.

The one thing you will learn, if you haven't already, is that the only thing keeping you from the high average you're capable of is your mental approach to the game.

If you have bowled for any length of time, you know all you need to know about the fundamentals of the delivery. If you are a beginner, it will take only a few weeks to learn the rudiments from a competent instructor at your local lanes. Your problem is putting into practice what you know is the best and most effective delivery for a big pin fall.

With self-hypnosis, you will learn how to control your tensions. It will allow you, like the champions, to take your practice game into league play.

The reason this promise can be held out to you so confidently is in the explanation of self-hypnosis given by Dr. Frank S. Caprio, an eminent Washington psychiatrist. He says, "Self-hypnosis is the means by which a normal person may relieve tensions, inspire confidence and add zest to living."

The application of this to your bowling game was explained by Joseph Whitney in his popular King Features syndicated newspaper column, "Mirror of Your Mind." He wrote: "Properly performed, hypnosis is capable of changing mental attitudes at the conscious level. If faulty mental attitudes are responsible for an athlete's inadequate performance, a change wrought by hypnosis could improve his skill."

The promise for better bowling is simply this: WITH UNDERSTANDING AND PROPER APPLICATION OF SELF-HYPNOSIS, YOU WILL BE ABLE TO BOWL THE BEST GAME YOU ARE PHYSICALLY CAPABLE OF PLAYING.

Chapter 2

It's Brains, Not Brawn

NO MUSCLES NEEDED

You may think the "joker" in the promise for better bowling is that it has been limited to "the best game you are physically capable of playing."

However, it was phrased that way because self-hypnosis embodies the mental side of bowling. If you are anywhere near average physically, you have all the muscles needed to roll the ball down the lane. Bowling doesn't require any more strength than that needed to lift a ball weighing anywhere from 10 to 16 pounds.

In West Palm Beach, Florida, Marie Grupi, 7, has a 112 average. Ron Parmenter, 15, of Seattle, Washington, has carried a 180 average for several years and Jan Seiden of North Miami, Florida, rolled a 678 series when he was 9 years old. At the ripe age of 11, he has a 170 average.

Joseph Smentkowski bowled a 300 game on his 70th

birthday. Ebber (Sarge) Easter, at 67, was a member of the Detroit Pepsi Cola team that won the 1950 ABC championship. The same year he paired with Ed Lubanski to pick up the National Doubles Match Game title.

Marion Ladewig is a 45-year-old grandmother weighing 125 pounds, who has a 20-year average of 190 and has collected 14 national titles. Sylvia Wene is 4'11" and a Bowling Proprietor's Association of America all-star champion with a 206 average.

A great many physically handicapped individuals can do well at bowling. Johnny Roos is a polio paraplegic with his body almost complete encased in braces who rolls to a 134 average. Ziggy Malinowski is 97 percent blind and has a 163 average with a 638 series and a 244 high game.

It's as All-Star Buddy Bomar says, "It's not how many muscles you have that counts, it's how you use them."

Every instructor cautions that the "speed ball" is much too difficult to control to be effective. Throwing the ball too fast causes it to skid and there's no way of telling when the break will come. The steady bowlers use a full roller and it requires no more muscles than it takes to lift the ball and swing it easily.

THE FALLACY OF CONCENTRATION

The mental side of bowling is most commonly thought of and described as tension, freezing or steering the ball. It is 100 percent mental.

Your muscles are capable of the easy, smooth delivery so necessary for high scoring. Your practice games have already proved that. It's the interference of their performance by your mind that causes the jerky, uncoordinated release that defeats you.

You can make a test to prove the above statement without going to a bowling lane or holding a ball. If you are seated in a chair as you read this, think for a moment on what kind of muscle action it would take you to get up.

How far will you bend forward before applying pressure from your hands and arms to assist in lifting your body? What leg muscles will you use? Now, as you're coming out of the chair, how will you maintain your balance? How are you going to use your feet, legs and body to get in an erect position?

Think about this for several minutes. Then, try consciously to concentrate on one movement at a time — bending your back, lifting with your arms, pushing with your legs and balancing with your feet. If you do this deliberately, without allowing the natural movement, you may find it very difficult to get out of the chair.

One of the most difficult physical movements for an individual, according to anatomists, is the simple act of climbing a flight of stairs. It brings into play almost every muscle and bone in the body to keep the person in balance. It is much more difficult than the physical movements required for rolling a bowling ball.

"But how about holding the ball in one hand with only the fingers?" you ask. "Doesn't that put you out of balance? Isn't that the real problem in getting a smooth delivery?"

The answer is you walked from your car to the bowling lanes holding the bag with your ball, didn't you? Did you feel out of balance or uncomfortable?

"But that's different," you counter. "Walking is natural. It's harder to keep your balance when you have to concentrate on getting the ball in the 1-3 pocket."

Concentrate on what? The stance? The placement of the feet? Shoulders square to the line? The pushaway? The stepoff and backswing? The in-line steps to the foul line? The straight arm delivery? The release with a lift to impart spin for the hook? The pins, spot or line for your aim? How many things are there to concentrate upon and how many things can you think about in the time it takes from the pushaway to the release?

Of course, there's no argument about good bowling requiring concentration. You can't stand up there with a blank mind or in a fog and wish the ball down the lane. And just let your attention wander and you're sunk.

IT'S THE SUBCONSCIOUS FEEL YOU WANT

At this point, it may appear contradictory and confusing to try to follow the advice of the experts, namely, that good form for the delivery requires relaxation and at the same time concentration. The two actions may appear to be opposites.

If you have tried to follow the advice to relax and still found yourself gripping the ball too tightly, or starting off with a jerky foot movement and losing control of the delivery in the backswing, you know there has to be something more. It's that indefinable something that comes to you every so often during a practice session when things seem to go just right.

It's that subconscious feel. The muscle movement is directed subconsciously just as it is when you are walking.

"But how do I get this feeling when I want it?" you ask. "What good does it do me to be a champ in practice and a chump in league play?"

You will learn to activate the subconscious feel through self-hypnosis. Further, you will discover that this smooth, coordinated muscle movement is best accomplished in competition through the use of self-hypnosis.

SELF-HYPNOSIS WILL SHOW YOU HOW TO TAKE YOUR PRACTICE GAMES INTO LEAGUE PLAY.

Chapter 3

Your Subconscious And Its Application For Better Bowling

WHAT'S GOOD FORM?

As a serious student of the game, how do you determine what will be the best form for you to use? Exactly what is good bowling form?

If you are a beginner, should you start with the two or three-finger ball? If you've been at the game a long time and haven't improved the way you would like, would it help to change from a four-step to a five-step approach? Maybe your backswing is too high, or you aren't coming in low enough for the release. Should you try to get more of a hook, or is the curved ball more dependable?

Every bowler wonders about his form. As he watches the good Classic league players smash out strikes at his home lane or watches the television stars rack up 200-plus games, he wonders if there isn't some tip he can pick up from their technique that will improve his own game.

Take this tip from Champion Ned Day. "If you are really interested in your game, you should watch some of the top players in action. You may see something you particularly admire in another's form which you would like to adapt to your own game. On the other hand, don't try to copy a star's form completely. If you do, the style may not fit you. Bowling is a game where you must be natural, so be yourself at all times."

Beyond the fundamentals which a bowler learns in a very short time, it isn't what form you use that counts. It's how you use it.

Dick Weber, who introduced the unique thumb glove and has collected a notable number of championships, warns: "Don't try to copy anybody's game style. Develop and build your own form. Above all, keep relaxed. Co-ordination and timing are the keys to this game."

There is only one "must" in bowling. That is to release the ball so that it rolls down the lane in a certain path to reach the 1-3 pocket of the pin set. How you arrive at this position for release is a highly individual matter. Few sports allow such a diversity of form. But at the same time, few sports require such precision timing and coordination for good results.

THE STARS ARE INDIVIDUALS

There are a great many champions who are living proof that there isn't any single style or even combination of styles that can be labeled as the best or right for everyone.

Don Carter, Brunswick advisory staff member and four-times All-Star champion, has called himself the "wrongest" bowler. He violates the presumably all-important straight arm delivery by deliberately bending his arm at the elbow.

"I don't advocate the bent elbow for anyone else," Carter says. "It just happens to suit me." But there is one bit of advice Carter does think is valuable. "When things don't go right, or you get a 10-pin tap when you think you deserved a clean strike, don't lose your temper. Anger makes you tense and above all you must be relaxed to bowl."

Lee Jouglard, one of bowling's all-time greats who held the 10-year best average, teaches the four-step approach and uses the three-step for his own game. Eddie Lubanski tells his pupils to use the three-finger ball and uses a two-finger ball. With it, he put two 300 games back-to-back on a television series.

Johnny King, an AMF advisory staff member, who could fill a trunk with trophies and makes a good living from competition and teaching bowling, uses a five-step approach with practically no backswing for a full roller with a sharp break. Johnny doesn't advise his students to copy his style. "Most bowlers find a moderate backswing and the four-step the best delivery. But for me, I find the less I wave the ball around in the air, the better it is," he says.

Carmen Salvino twists the ball in his grip and pays no attention to the supposedly cardinal rule of the firm wrists. Students are often cautioned about powering the ball, yet Claude (Pat) Patterson, an ABC medal winner with an all-time high average in BPAA Match game team play, uses a speed ball with an exceptionally high backswing. Another who likes a fast ball is the "Grand Old Man" of the game, Andy Varipapa, who started bowling in 1905 and was elected to the Bowling Hall of Fame in 1957.

Then, there's "Wrong Foot" Lou Campi. Lou ends his delivery on his right foot. The average bowler trying this approach would receive correction from his teammates and a warning he would never learn to bowl successfully. Campi received the same advice when he began bowling at 32 years of age. But he brought with him the form he had used as a youngster to play Bocci, the Italian version of bowling, in which the players take three steps and finish on their right foot. But with this form, Campi has collected just about every title offered in bowling.

There are hundreds of other examples that could be cited as proof of just one thing. To master bowling, you have to be natural. The moment you try to contort yourself into some style for an effect, you're whipped.

RHYTHM IS THE SECRET

The answer to why there is such a variation of style among championship caliber players is simple. Few ever took a lesson to learn how to play the game. They learned to bowl by bowling. They experimented until they found what was comfortable and effective and then practiced it until it became second nature.

Deliberately trying to copy an uncomfortable individual movement requires the restriction of a natural muscle movement and this creates tension. It may stand up for a short time, but as the tension increases or decreases, the form will vary and the bowling become erratic.

Ed Kawolics, another champion who uses the two-finger ball, emphasizes this by saying: "Nobody can tell you how to stand, how much to bend or how big a back-swing you should take. The only measure is the way you feel and you judge this by whether or not you are comfortable and relaxed."

Women bowlers, and there are now more than three million, receive the same advice from Marion Ladewig, who has been given the honorary title, "Queen of Bowling." She says, "Bowling isn't a matter of strength. Its success is in timing and rhythm. And because most women are better dancers than men, once they get the feeling of this rhythm, they become good players."

Sylvia Wene has put it in almost the same words, "Sure, men have more muscles but ladies have better rhythm and timing. These are the prime requisites for good bowling."

Among the top bowlers in the nation, you will find tall ones and short ones, fat and skinny, young and old. Their styles vary but they have one thing in common — the ability to roll the ball into that 1-3 pocket or come back with a spare when they fail to get the strike. And all of them credit their success to timing and rhythm.

WHERE DO YOU FIND RHYTHM?

"I'm convinced," you may say. "The form I have may be okay. But what causes me to be so inconsistent? One time I roll the ball into the pocket for a clean sweep. The next time I completely miss the head pin. I pick up a tough combination for a spare and drop the ball in the gutter going for a lone 10 pin. Something's wrong with my game or I'd have a lot better average than I now hold."

There's something wrong, all right. It's your mental approach. This doesn't mean that you aren't capable of the right mental approach to bowling. It does mean that you haven't discovered what you need to put your game together solidly.

Think back to the practice session when you had the feeling you had found the secret to good bowling. Try to recall the sensation you had with the smooth approach that sent the ball on its way to the coveted pocket.

There's a good chance you will say, "As far as I can remember, I didn't feel a thing. If it is at all possible to describe, I'd say you could best liken it to an actual lack of feeling."

Exactly! That's subconscious feel.

Whenever there is tension, the muscles are taut. The muscles are controlled by nerves and the nerves directed by the mind. So when there's a conflict of direction, as in tension, the muscles work against each other and there's a feeling of strain. When they are allowed free movement, working normally, there's no strain. That's rhythm.

Could you describe any particular muscle feeling you might have while walking, waving your hand, driving a car, feeding yourself or any of the myriad activities which are a normal part of your everyday existence?

This muscle rhythm which the experts describe as coordination and timing is nothing more than allowing the muscles to be directed subconsciously without any conscious interference.

TENSION IS MENTAL INTERFERENCE

Compare your normal physical and mental activity of walking into the bowling center with that you undergo while taking your bowling approach. You managed to walk in, take your assigned lane, bend over to put on your shoes and all the other things without feeling any strain.

But as you pick up your ball to take your stance, you start to tell yourself, "Got to get my feet lined up." So you shuffle into position and anchor them there. "Hand under the ball and wrist firm," you go on. "And remember to push it away about chest high." As you are about to start, the thought flashes into your mind about holding the line while keeping the backswing to a minimum and bringing the ball in close to your body with a pendulum motion. "Don't forget to slide," is another direction, with a final warning about the lift on the release to produce spin, to watch the spot or pins and not to cross the foul line.

Do you honestly think if you went through that mental ritual each time you took a step up a flight of stairs you could get to the top without stumbling?

"How else can I learn to bowl if I don't follow a set pattern and stick to it?" you ask. "If I don't keep my mind on what I'm doing, I don't get anywhere."

Well, that's what you are going to learn from the use of self-hypnosis. You will learn to commit all of these details to your subconscious. They will become as automatic as walking, lifting a cup of coffee or writing your name.

When automatic movements are made, they are controlled subconsciously. Your conscious mind does not interfere and there is no conflict set up which creates tension.

SELF-HYPNOSIS WILL SHOW YOU THE MEANS OF RIDDING YOURSELF OF MENTAL INTERFERENCE WITH NATURAL AND NORMAL MUSCLE MOVEMENTS.

Chapter 4

Good Bowlers Use Mental Discipline

THE END RESULT

The subconscious feel occurs when the subconscious mind directs muscle movements to produce an end result in the conscious mind.

When you consciously think of drinking from a cup, your conscious mind does not direct all the muscle activity necessary to produce the end result. It gives a single command and the subconscious mind produces all the muscle movements necessary to grip the cup handle with your fingers, lift it to your lips and swallow.

In all normal physical activities, the conscious mind thinks only of the end result. In walking, it doesn't direct the feet or body balance. In writing, it thinks of words and the subconscious mind directs the movements to produce the letters.

That's what you must have for coordination and timing in bowling. You must learn how to let the conscious mind direct the end result of the delivery, while the subconscious mind takes over all the correct mechanical motions to produce the end result.

The subconscious direction will coordinate the individual movements of taking your stance, the pushaway, backswing, slide and release with the same natural rhythm you use in walking down the street, stepping off the curb, by-passing an obstacle and then stepping back up on the sidewalk.

When the movements of your delivery become automatic and repetitive, you can perform them time and again in an identical manner to produce the same end result.

WHY SELF-HYPNOSIS?

You may ask, "Why do I need self-hypnosis for bowling? I've learned to walk, drink, write my name and climb stairs without self-hypnosis. What is the difference between these automatic movements and those in bowling?"

There are two reasons for using self-hypnosis for bowling.

First, you will be able to train your subconscious memory to produce these automatic movements more quickly with hypnosis and learn how to trigger the response for the subconscious feel. This is a technique to speed up the normal learning period.

Second, and more important, is that whenever a penalty is involved in an action, the conscious mind will interfere with the normal subconscious action.

For a demonstration, let's suppose you have had a cup of coffee in the living room. You take the cup and saucer back to the kitchen. It's an ordinary cup and saucer and you carry it without thinking about it and with no trouble.

However, suppose instead of an ordinary cup and saucer, it is a very valuable piece of china that belongs to your host. You know that it's irreplaceable and if you should bump into anything and drop it, you'd be in an embarrassing position. You are consciously aware of the penalty for your action. You will feel the tension gather in your hands, arms and body as you carry it into the kitchen.

A more dramatic illustration is used by psychologists who suggest you would have no trouble with subconscious muscle direction in walking a narrow plank laid on the ground. If you raised the same plank high in the air between two tall buildings, and with your conscious mind aware of the penalty for falling, it would not allow you to move a muscle.

YOU "FREEZE" BECAUSE YOU'RE AFRAID

It is this same "freeze" or muscle tension that raises havoc with your bowling delivery. It keeps you from employing the smooth form with which you roll the ball in practice in your league play.

During practice, you were concerned only with perfecting your form. The pin count was not a factor. There was no penalty involved for failure. In league play or competition, the score is the penalty. The conscious mind takes over to assist and the interference with the subconscious movements sets up tension.

"But I'm not actually afraid," you say. "I've been bowling in a league for a long time. It doesn't upset me to have a crowd around. And I don't get angry even when I get a lousy break out of a pocket hit and get stuck with an impossible split."

The fear doesn't need to be great enough to cause you to shake or perspire. It needs to be only enough to cause you concern over the result so that it interferes with the normal subconscious movements.

There are degrees of tension. You might not become so concerned that your fingers would literally freeze in the ball and your joints become inoperative. But a lesser degree of tension can make you erratic, or as Falcaro warned: "With a 300 game in the offing, relaxation turns to tension and muscles tighten. The ball seems to get heavier and more difficult to release."

That's why turkeys are so hard to come by. Your conscious mind becomes aware of the big 30 count. Hank Marino, in his instruction book, says: "Relaxation, a looseness of muscles and freedom of mind, is a must. There can be no conflicting thoughts once the stance is taken. Some people think that stiffening the arm produces tension, while actually the reverse is true. It's tension that stiffens the arm and hinders a smooth delivery."

WHAT TO DO ABOUT IT

If the conscious mind, aware of a penalty, produces muscle tension, what can you do about it?

"It's already been pointed out you just can't stand up there in a fog," you say. "How can I possibly keep from being aware of the score and a desire to come through with a strike when that's the whole object of the game?"

Superficially, it would appear to be a moot question. But there is an answer and that is discovering some means of distracting the conscious mind during the bowling delivery so that it is unaware of the consequences or penalty involved in the action.

That can be done only with hypnosis. And that's the reason for the statement that good bowling can best be accomplished with the use of self-hypnosis. There's no better way to relieve tension.

"Do you mean to say all good bowlers, even the tournament stars, use self-hypnosis?" you ask. "If that's true, how come I haven't heard about it before? I can't recall anyone saying they were using hypnosis in bowling."

They use self-hypnosis, all right. They may be unaware of the term, for it's only been within the past few years that hypnosis has been recognized by the American Medical Association. Being unfamiliar with the phenomenon, the stars have tried to pass on what they have found in such vague terms as relaxation, coordination and rhythm. They are actually describing the result, rather than how it is obtained.

SELF-HYPNOSIS IS THE ONLY ANSWER

Let's take an example from Ned Day's exceptionally fine book, *How To Bowl Better*. When it comes to the mental side of the game, he writes: "Bowling is a game of smoothness, balance, poise and skill, requiring the coordination of all muscles, rather than just the strenuous use of one set of them. The player must avoid tension at all costs."

But how do you avoid tension? You can't consciously will yourself to be relaxed. You've probably found that out. The more you try to relax, the more tense you become. The reason is that you are increasing the conscious penalty by placing a premium on relaxation as well as the score.

Some players feel that a drink or two will relax them. Alcohol only produces an illusion of competence. Actually, it destroys the one means of obtaining relaxation, namely, concentration of the conscious mind upon an object or thought which does not involve a penalty.

YOU WILL DISCOVER, AS YOU UNDERSTAND THE MENTAL PROCESS INVOLVED IN SELF-HYPNOSIS, THAT IT IS THE BEST "HOW TO" INSTRUCTION FOR RELAXATION, COORDINATION, RHYTHM AND TIMING.

Chapter 5

Use Your Subconscious For Better Bowling

YOU HAVE TWO MINDS

The simplest explanation for the phenomenon of hypnosis, both as to what it is and what it can do, is an understanding of the relationship between the conscious and subconscious minds.

Possibly, until now, you have considered your mind as singular, simply referring to it as the brain. The brain is the organic part of the intellect. The mind refers to the use of the brain. Technically, there are several parts to the brain, but for the need at hand it is sufficient to consider it as being in only two parts, the conscious and subconscious.

The conscious mind directs all reasoned action.

The subconscious mind controls automatic responses.

The conscious mind has been termed the "new mind," or the "mind of man." By using its reasoning power, man, if he wishes, may direct his own destiny. He can evaluate by applying reasoning to experience and knowledge for a logical answer.

The subconscious mind, often called the "old mind," is the memory for the conscious mind. It is the storehouse for facts, instincts and motivations. Man shares it with all other creatures, even to the smallest insects.

The subconscious mind responds with conditioned instincts. A dog shies from a stick and a man jumps when he hears a sudden, loud noise, not through reasoning, but from conditioned fear in the subconscious mind.

The subconscious mind has no power to reason and there is a purpose in this. If it could reason and change the facts stored in its memory, the conscious mind would have no source to consult for the truth upon which to base its reasoning for logic.

IT'S THAT SIMPLE

The basic theory of hypnosis is the fact that the conscious mind has the exclusive power to reason and the subconscious has no power to reason and accepts everything it receives as truth.

"This seems to be getting a long way from the bowling lane and my delivery," you say.

Is it? What are you looking for to improve your bowling? Would a coordinated, repetitive delivery that sends the ball down the lane in the same pattern time after time solve your problems?

If during practice you can train the subconscious mind to direct muscle movements for the correct bowling form, it must repeat them exactly as given whenever it is called upon by the conscious mind since the subconscious cannot alter any direction it receives.

Isn't this exactly how you learned to walk, talk, play a musical instrument, drive a car, use a typewriter or any of the other subconsciously controlled muscle movements? You consciously directed the movements until they became firmly established in the memory pattern of the subconscious mind. All that is needed to trigger them for the end result is a single thought in the conscious mind.

You no longer think of the gas throttle, the brake pedal, the gear shift or the steering wheel to drive an automobile. You have no need to consciously direct the movements of your feet and hands. They respond automatically to a single conscious desire to drive.

This is what Carmen Salvino had in mind when he said, "I practice until the game becomes automatic. I don't have to think about what I intend to do with the ball so that I can be completely relaxed and natural when I am in competition."

With the subconscious mind trained to produce a physical action that would coordinate all of the muscles to send the ball down the lane time after time into the strike pocket, there would be almost unlimited improvement. Of course, the human body isn't machine perfect. And there are times when an apparently good pocket hit will produce a tap to leave a pin. But the goal is to become as near perfect as possible.

TENSION IS THE VILLAIN

There's only one thing that spoils this perfect plan to have the subconscious mind control the bowling delivery. It is interference by the conscious mind to produce tension.

The subconscious mind, without power of reasoning, can't change the memory pattern it has been given. But the conscious mind can change it. The conscious mind can call into play whatever muscles it wishes and at whatever time it commands them.

It might be well to determine exactly what tension is and why it is produced.

Tension is the contraction of muscles. The action is controlled by the nerves which are directed from the mind. When you wish to close your hand, your mind sends the message through the nerves. It contracts the muscles in your fingers to pull them closed. To open your hand, another set of muscles is activated to pull the fingers open.

But if the first set, which closed the fingers, fails to relax, the second set to open the hand works against them and there is a strain. This is tension where muscles work against each other. The effect is to make various joints and sockets in the bone structure immovable.

It accounts for the statement that a person can become literally "scared stiff." All of the muscles working against each other produce complete tension.

WHY DO YOU DO IT

A person isn't going to deliberately ruin his bowling delivery by producing tension when he is fully aware that the best results can be obtained from relaxation and coordination.

Tension is created by fear.

When there is a penalty involved in an action, the conscious mind becomes fearful that the subconscious mind will not perform to perfection. It assists by giving additional direction to the muscles, which sets up counteractions and the muscles work against each other producing strain.

Suppose you were awakened from a deep sleep and heard a strange noise in your home. You would feel yourself become tense. This is because the conscious mind is alerting all muscles to be ready for action. The result is they are contracted just a little to produce the tension.

This is what happens when a driver freezes at the wheel of his car with an accident impending, or when a person with stage fright finds he cannot use his vocal chords.

In bowling, your conscious mind becomes aware of the score. It wants the best possible effort and is aware of the penalty if the ball goes wide, fails to hook, or crosses over too quickly. It no longer trusts the subconscious delivery, so it starts to "help" with the grip and tightens up the fingers. It helps the arms, feet and legs and tightens them up. As added insurance, instead of allowing the ball to be rolled, it issues a command to steer it. And you are well aware of what this conscious help does to your game. You get the wooden Indian with the cannon ball feeling.

HYPNOSIS IS THE SOLUTION

What can you do about it? Obviously, since at all times the conscious mind is aware of a penalty, it will produce tension. The only answer is to concentrate the conscious mind upon a thought or action that does not involve a penalty. When this concentration, which is actually distraction, takes place, the conscious mind has no thought of fear and will allow the subconscious to control the muscle action.

Concentration of the conscious mind to distract it is one of the techniques used by hypnotists to place a subject in a hypnotic state.

"You mean, I am going to bowl while I'm hypnotized," you ask.

Definitely, no! That is a fallacy that has caused much confusion about the application of self-hypnosis to sports. You will be in a light hypnotic state in the privacy of your home while practicing self-hypnosis. During actual play or practice you will only trigger your subconscious mind to take control of the automatic response of the bowling delivery. It's as natural and normal as walking. You practice this use of subconscious control in your daily routine of living. What is new is to be aware of it. And to learn the means by which you can trigger this automatic response by a conscious command.

A very apt description of self-hypnosis has been given by Dr. Milton Erickson, dean of the American medical hypnotists. He says, "Self-hypnosis plays a valuable role in a process which makes it easier for an individual to discover and understand the workings of his own body and mind and the factors which basically cause his own distress."

YOU WILL LEARN TO USE SELF-HYPNOSIS TO CONTROL THE TENSIONS AND JITTERS THAT HAVE KEPT YOU FROM BOWLING TO THE BEST OF YOUR ABILITY. THE METHOD OF ACCOMPLISHING THIS WILL BE AS NORMAL AS THE AUTOMATIC RESPONSE WHILE WALKING.

Chapter 6

What You Should Know About Self-Hypnosis

YOU CAN'T WILL RELAXATION

If we are agreed tension is keeping you from bowling your best, and since the experts are in universal agreement on this point, let's see what can be done to get rid of it.

Instruction books and instructors usually by-pass any attempt to explain how you should relax. They simply state you must be relaxed and let it go at that. When an explanation is given, it's usually in such vague terms as "get your muscles loosened up," or "develop a free and easy style."

This is about as valuable as telling a person with insomnia to go to sleep, or someone with an emotional problem to stop worrying. The only way to eliminate tension is to eliminate the cause of tension.

In fact, the suggestion that you should try to relax is actually harmful. The harder you try to consciously relax, the more tense you become.

You may be aware of this from personal experience. Have you ever tried to force yourself to sleep, knowing you had a hard day ahead of you, only to find the more you tried the more wide awake you became? That's what happens when you consciously will yourself to relax.

There's an explanation for what takes place in your mind when you consciously will an effort. The conscious mind is in control of the muscles and nerves and alerts them, thus producing tension.

In the case of sleep, it is the fear that if you do not sleep you will not be rested enough to do your best the following day. You may recall as you tried to force yourself to sleep that the muscles in your neck, back, arms and legs became taut, making sleep impossible. In bowling, it is the fear that if you tighten up you won't roll the ball smoothly. The more concerned you are, the more tension results.

YOU BY-PASS THE CONSCIOUS MIND

"If I can't tell myself to relax, how can I relax?" you ask. "It sounds like some kind of riddle."

The cause of tension is fear. You may prove this for yourself. If you tighten the muscles in your hand and forearm to make them rigid and tense, the muscles tire quickly and you relax them. But when fear produces the tension, even though you may be unaware of the source, the muscles can remain taut until they become strained enough to produce pain. Many persons suffer nervous backaches, headaches, stiff necks and pseudoarthritic pains from this cause.

Self-hypnosis will enable you to remove the cause of tension, which is conscious fear. Let's examine the phenomenon and see why it has been claimed that only with self-hypnosis is it possible to relax when a penalty is involved in an action.

There is nothing abnormal or mysterious about hypnosis. Its application is based solely on the known psychological relationship between the conscious and the subconscious minds. The subconscious, having no power to reason, accepts and acts upon any fact or suggestion given to it by the conscious mind.

The hypnotist asks the subject to uncritically accept suggestions so that the reasoning, analytic qualities of the mind are suspended and the suggestion goes unchanged to the subconscious. Of course, this presupposes that the hypnotist will make helpful suggestions. The conscious mind will always reject anything foreign to its normal feelings.

This technique of hypnosis is the method used to bypass the conscious mind. It is strengthened by concentrating the conscious attention upon a single object or thought.

An illustration is the dentist using hypnosis who tells a patient he will feel no pain. Without hypnosis, the patient's conscious mind would reject the suggestion. Under hypnosis, the conscious mind accepts the statement and the subconscious mind records there will be no pain. The subconscious mind cannot challenge nor alter the suggestion, so the patient is unable to feel pain.

The depth of hypnosis is dependent upon increased suggestibility. The hypnotist requests the person to concentrate his attention upon a whirling disc, a flashing light or some object that will tire his vision. He then suggests the subject relax. He tells him his lids are becoming heavy and his eyes will close. With each suggestion the person accepts without a conscious challenge, the more directly the hypnotist can establish a contact with the subconsious mind.

IT'S AN EVERY DAY EXPERIENCE

Very likely, you have experienced hypnosis without being aware of it. Have you ever been reading, watching television or engrossed with your thoughts and had someone speak to you? Your concentration was deep enough so that you were unaware of what was said. Yet, the sound was there. The message was picked up by your ears and given directly to your subconscious mind, without any conscious awareness.

A simple test can be made by coming upon someone deeply engrossed and in a commanding voice, give the order: "Stand up!" If the direction is firm enough, the person will rise, and only after he is standing will he question the reason. The command was received and acted upon by the subconscious mind, while the conscious mind was concentrated on something else.

Have you ever driven your car over a familiar route while engrossed with your thoughts? You may go a considerable distance without being consciously aware of driving or seeing the landscape. The subconscious mind took over all of the driving while the conscious mind was concentrated upon other problems.

You may have heard or said, "It always seems shorter coming back than going." On the way to your destination, your conscious mind is concerned with the route. On the way back, it relegates the familiar route to your subconscious mind and is engrossed with other thoughts.

Many every day experiences with hypnosis could be cited, from putting on your clothes in the morning while your conscious thoughts are upon something else to using the tools with which you work without consciously being aware of the physical activity in using them.

THE BOWLING STARS USE SELF-HYPNOSIS

Now, as to whether or not the bowling stars use self-hypnosis (regardless of what they call it), the following was related by Dick Weber, a member of the famous Budweiser team. Weber collected the 1957 all-star crown and was named professional bowler of the year in 1959.

In a magazine articles, Weber wrote: "Above all, a bowler must keep relaxed. Coordination and timing are the keys to this game and you lose both if you tense up. One way to do this is to concentrate exclusively on your own game, or even the one frame you're bowling at any given time. Don't let your thoughts wander.

"I never could do this myself, until I learned a funny lesson. It was in 1956, and I was bowling against Don Carter in the All-Star finals. I suddenly became aware that Carter wouldn't talk to me or look at me during play. I couldn't figure it out. After all, we were teammates.

"When it was all over, I didn't ask him about it, thinking he was angry at something I had said or done. But during the months that followed, I watched him more closely, and I finally realized that it was just a matter of concentration. He'd been so absorbed in his game that he had no room in his attention for anything else.

"Once I learned to concentrate this way, my bowling began to improve rapidly."

Like most advice concerning the mental phase of the game, Weber left unanswered what it was he and Carter had learned to concentrate their attention upon. It couldn't have been any particular part of their bowling form or delivery, otherwise the results would have been exactly opposite. Instead of gaining coordination and timing, conscious attention to form or delivery would have produced tension.

Joe Wilman, in his very popular syndicated newspaper column on bowling instruction, "Joe Wilman's Bowling," said: "When I teach a beginning bowler to improve his game, there's one problem that they all seem to have in common — regardless of how much bowling experience they might have. The problem is tension which can tighten the muscles and cause two common mistakes. One is a jerky arm swing and the other is squeezing the ball."

But as to how to relieve tension, Wilman only offers: "So, when you find the nerves tightening, stop and relax a bit. Put the ball down, if necessary. Then, relax, let 'er roll."

However, in another article which he titled, "Ride Hot Streak, Don't Analyze It," Wilman came very close to describing both the technique and the application of self-hypnosis.

"Hot streaks for bowlers are just as much a part of the game as cold streaks. They happen to every bowler—but not often enough, of course.

"Many bowlers will prematurely kill a hot streak by trying to analyze it too closely while it is in progress. It's only natural to want to know what you're doing right so you can continue to do it, but often such analyzing can ruin the delicate timing that makes such a hot streak possible.

"I never make any changes when I'm bowling well. And I don't check my technique too closely, either. I note my starting position and my finishing position. And I also watch the path of my ball, so I can make sure that my ball will follow the same path each time.

"I'm a firm believer in not tampering with success. And when you're in a hot streak, ride it for all you're worth, without doing anything to end it."

In other words, Wilman expertly advises to concentrate conscious attention away from the physical movements of the delivery to allow the subconscious to control the muscle movements.

YOU CAN STILL BE FRIENDLY AND CONCENTRATE

The word concentration is often misused and misunderstood. It is confused with will power. You can't consciously will yourself to relax because will power engages the conscious mind to direct the action. The conscious mind alerts the nerves and muscles and produces the tension you are trying to avoid.

However, concentrating the conscious attention upon a thought or action that is not involved with the mechanics of bowling, as it is done in hypnosis, distracts the conscious mind and allows the subconscious to perform its normal duties.

The only time this distraction is necessary is from the time you take your stance on the approach until you have completed your delivery.

Much of the pleasure in bowling is the companionship and camaraderie with the other players on your team and in your league. There is no necessity to shut yourself out completely from this part of the fun and fellowship.

Mistakenly, because they are unaware of the mental process involved, some players believe they must remain in deep concentration throughout the entire game or series. Using self-hypnosis, you will learn how to concentrate your conscious attention and trigger the subconscious release only during the time you are actively engaged in delivering the ball.

It has been suggested that the rarity of 300 games in the ABC tournaments in which the greatest bowlers participate is because of the extreme tension. Billy Knox scored the first one in 1913 and there was a 13-year wait until Charlie Reinlie duplicated the feat.

Most of the perfect games have been scored in single game or double play, leading many observers to believe team competition, which progresses at a slower pace, creates such tension that the potential 300 bowler is more apt to become a victim of mounting pressure. Up until 1958, there hadn't been a single 300 game rolled in team play in the ABC tournaments.

Using self-hypnosis, the player will learn how to "throw the switch" on his conscious mind, which builds up these pressures during competition, and activate the subconscious feel to give himself the relaxed form needed.

YOU WILL FIND THAT YOUR BOWLING PLEASURE IS GREATLY INCREASED BY USING SELF-HYPNOSIS, NOT ONLY FROM A SCORING STANDPOINT, BUT BECAUSE BETWEEN FRAMES YOU WILL NOT BE WORRIED OR CONCERNED ABOUT YOUR NEXT DELIVERY.

Chapter 7

Here's The Real Secret For Better Bowling

ALL GOOD ATHLETES DISCOVER SUBCONSCIOUS FEEL

Have you noticed how quickly athletes from other sports become adept at bowling? Baseball players score well soon after they have learned the basic fundamentals. Mickey Mantle, Stan Musial, Duke Snider and Yogi Berra all enjoy bowling and maintain good averages. Football quarterbacks Bobby Layne of the Pittsburgh Steelers and Johnny Unitas of the Baltimore Colts are good bowlers.

Many bowling stars are also exceptionally fine golfers and vice versa.

It is because they bring to every game that subconscious feel that affords the necessary relaxation.

Every sport requires timing and coordination, whether it's golf, trapshooting or skiing. Those who master the sport discover the way to let their subconscious control the muscle movements for whatever mechanical movements are required.

PRACTICE MAKES PERFECT

Practice is stressed in every sport. In some sports it is required to build strength to withstand the strenuous effort. This isn't a prime requisite for bowling, as it doesn't require any great physical strength to roll the ball down the lane.

Another phase of practice is called "muscle training" or "muscle memory." What is sought is an automatic response to produce the correct muscle movement repeatedly for a certain result. Baseball players have batting practice for hours on end. Skating stars practically live at the rink. Basketball players toss the ball endlessly at the hoop.

Long after the muscles required to perform the action are developed to full strength, the practice continues. And while the practice is a physical effort, what actually is being accomplished is a habit pattern—which is mental.

Muscles have no memory. They are directed in their action by nerves in response to a mental command. The purpose of training is to deeply record in the subconscious mind the memory of every nerve commanded to produce the ultimate coordinated physical action.

Any muscle movement must first be learned consciously. A child learns to walk by consciously imitating his elders. At first, it is haltingly, then as the movements become firmly implanted in the subconscious memory, it becomes an automatic response.

This is your ultimate goal in practice for bowling. Condition your subconscious mind for all the movements necessary to correctly deliver the ball along a path to the 1-3 pocket or to pick off any pins left and a tap or split. The ideal will be reached when this subconscious reflex can be triggered by a conscious command as readily as it is obtained for walking, writing, dancing or other automatic actions.

YOU LEARN TO FORGET

Think back a moment to the trouble you experienced when you were first learning to dance. You were consciously aware of the movement of your feet. You were trying to establish the pattern of the dance step.

Then, as the dance steps became automatic, you forgot about them and your feet. The movements were triggered by the rhythm of the music.

But first you consciously learned the steps. What you did about "forgetting" them was actually to entrust them to the subconscious memory. You dismissed them from your conscious mind.

And as your skill in dancing increased, you were able to dismiss the rhythm of the music from your conscious mind and carry on a conversation with your partner. The rhythm of the music became the trigger to activate the subconscious movement.

The important first step, however, was to consciously learn the correct movements. The subconscious mind must accept whatever it receives from the conscious mind without challenge or alteration. If you failed to learn the correct basic steps, you would never be able to perform them and become a good dancer.

Bowling allows a wide variance of individual styles for delivery, but there are basic fundamentals to be learned for good bowling form. Deliberately ignoring good bowling form would be like learning to walk pigeon-toed or dancing on your heels.

71

If you are a beginning bowler, this is especially important because once you have consciously learned the basic fundamentals, you will forget them as they are entrusted to the subconscious memory.

IT MUST BE NATURAL

If you have been bowling for any length of time, it should be easy to quickly adjust any flaws in your delivery. Warm up on a practice lane by rolling a few balls as naturally as possible, without any regard to the score.

It is a "must" that you completely disregard the pin fall. Otherwise, your conscious attention will be on the results rather than upon adjusting your style to make it completely natural.

After you have warmed up, check whether the various movements of the delivery feel free and easy. Is your backswing too high? Are you consciously trying to hold back? If you are trying to restrict your backswing, you are creating tensions which will defeat you. Or if you are taking too big a backswing, thinking to get more power into the delivery, you will have the same problem. Anything other than a natural movement brings into play additional muscles. They work against the normal muscle movement to create tension.

Possibly, you can get away with it for a time. By being consciously aware of a peculiarity foreign to the natural movement, you may be able to control it. But the moment there is a conscious mental lapse from this deliberate motion, it will be either increased or decreased and cause you to be erratic.

And it is absolutely impossible to use self-hypnosis for control if you persist in a deliberate unnatural muscle movement. For under hypnosis, the movement will be completely entrusted to the subconscious.

Go through your entire delivery, from stance and push-away to the release and follow through. If there is any part of it that seems unnatural or strained, it's very likely you are forcing yourself to copy some particular part of someone else's style.

No two bowlers are physically identical, nor do they have like temperaments. A big backswing and fast ball may be ideal for a teammate and all wrong for you. You will only know what is right for you when the movements in the delivery feel perfectly natural and without any muscle strain.

HOW TO MAKE CORRECTIONS

"What happens when I get a free and natural delivery but the pins don't fall?" you ask.

Remember, you were warned not to watch the score. The first thing is to get your delivery without any muscles working against each other. Each movement you make from the time you pick your ball up from the rack until it's well on its way down the lane is to be one coordinated effort.

But you've got that now. Let's see where the ball is rolling. Is it coming in too high? Or have you lost some of the hook and it's failing to curve into the 1-3 pocket? Should you make an adjustment to the lift to impart more spin, or lengthen the backswing for more speed?

POSITIVELY, NO! Once you have found a delivery that feels natural and is without any muscle strain, leave it that way. Unless you do, you will never bowl consistently. You will be making constant adjustments as the strain increases or decreases and you will never be able to form a memory pattern upon which you can rely. Every practice session will simply be another period of experimentation.

What you are seeking, and what you must have, is a delivery you can rely upon to perform the identical motions time and time again in exactly the same pattern.

The only adjustment you need to make, or will ever need to make once you have a "grooved" delivery, is where you take your stance to place yourself at a particular point at the foul line for release.

If the ball is crossing over too quickly, all you need is a wider approach. If it's coming in late, come in a little tighter. The swing and delivery remain in the groove.

You will readily appreciate the value of this if you should enter competition which will take you away from your home lanes. You will find because of lane construction or finish that some are faster or slower than others. The slow lane permits hooks readily while the fast one does not.

With your swing grooved and the delivery completely automatic, you will have no need to adjust any part of your game to compensate for the different lane speeds. All that is changed is the point of delivery, which can be quickly computed after rolling a few practice balls.

Ned Day in his book of bowling instruction stresses the grooved delivery. In commenting upon lane conditions, he says, "I know that at certain trying times you may feel that it must be necessary for you to roll more than one type of ball. Even in considering such cases, I stand on my original recommendation and advise that you exhaust every other possible means before abandoning your grooved delivery in favor of any radical change."

GO FOR THE SPARE WITH YOUR STRIKE BALL

Many bowlers completely change their delivery when going for spares. It is advisable, of course, to change the approach angle to lessen the margin of error, depending upon whether the remaining pin or pins are left on the right or left side of the lane.

BUT DON'T CHANGE YOUR GROOVED DELIVERY. If you can rely on it for the pocket strike, it will deliver for you in picking up the spares.

Some bowlers who use a hook or a curved ball delivery will "flatten out" going for a spare. This means you must either completely learn and commit to your subconscious memory two different bowling forms, or consciously change your natural style by interfering with the normal, coordinated movements. The latter is most often true, and by juggling back and forth between the two deliveries, you master neither of them.

Ned Day comments on this, saying: "It is true that there have been, and there still are, very fine bowlers who straighten out their hooks when bowling at certain types of spares. My contention has always been, however, that such bowlers might have been even better had they pursued the policy of remaining in the groove at all times."

The fewer adjustments you are forced to make in your game, once you have a natural, grooved delivery, the more completely you can rely upon its subconscious control. The more automatic it becomes, with the ball being delivered time after time in the same pattern, the more consistent you will become.

HOW LONG DOES IT TAKE?

How long it will take you to make these adjustments to

your game, to eliminate all the unnatural movements and develop a free and natural style, depends upon how readily you accept the theory that you must have a natural rhythm to become a good bowler.

The theory isn't new. It has been stressed by every bowling star and every bowling instructor. But many bowlers are reluctant to accept it, believing it is some twist or trick in the delivery that will give them proficiency.

A single session may show a vast improvement if you work at it sincerely. Any sign of muscle strain at any point in the delivery will tell you that the particular style does not quite fit you. Continue to make adjustments until the delivery flows smoothly, with a rhythm you might compare to dancing.

However, if your concern is still centered on the pin fall, even though it is a practice session, you may find it difficult to force yourself to relinquish deeply ingrained habits.

But once you have accepted the idea and have worked to develop your natural style, continued practice will show an increasing improvement in your bowling skill. There is only one caution. Be on the alert to sense the strain if it should creep back into your game.

Habits are hard to break. Until you have trained the subconscious memory through repeated practice and competition, they may gradually sneak back into your form. The one certain check is to go to a practice lane and see whether there is any muscle strain as you make the delivery.

RESIST THE TEMPTATION

There is one temptation that is difficult for most bowlers

to resist. It is to experiment with their natural form, hoping that some particular movement will miraculously send them soaring in the 200-plus bracket.

After watching someone who scores particularly well, they spot a peculiarity and say to themselves: "I wonder if that would work for me?"

They begin to experiment with a little more lift to the ball. It produces a sharper hook, so this necessitates more power and a bigger backswing and likely a change in the point of release. Before long, the "little experiment" has changed their entire game. "I don't know what happened," they complain. "I was coming along fine and now my entire game is wrecked."

Improvement, once you have a natural style, comes only from practice. The bowling stars put in from 50 to 60 practice games a week. How much time and money you can afford to spend on your bowling is an individual matter and in part is decided by how interested you are in becoming proficient.

Frank Clause wanted very much to become a top notch bowler. "I used to earn $75 a week as a school teacher," Clause said. "I spent almost every cent in a bowling alley." It has paid off big for Frank who is now a professional bowler.

THERE ARE TWO THINGS TO REMEMBER DURING PRACTICE. FORGET ABOUT THE PIN FALL. DON'T EXPERIMENT AFTER YOU HAVE A FREE, NATURAL STYLE. DEVOTE YOUR TIME TO PRACTICING IT SO THAT IT BECOMES COMPLETELY AUTOMATIC.

Chapter 8

How To Achieve Self-Hypnosis

TWO AIDS FOR IMPROVEMENT

In learning to induce self-hypnosis, you will accomplish two things to improve your bowling. The first will be to learn how to concentrate your conscious attention upon a single thought or object, which distracts it from any penalty involved in an action.

By this means, you will let the subconscious mind carry out its normal duties without conscious interference. You will do this at the time you are bowling, by triggering the subconscious mind with a conscious thought. It is what you do when you give yourself the command to walk, or any other subconsciously controlled act. It will result in an automatic, repetitive delivery for consistent high scoring.

Secondly, you will learn to induce self-hypnosis in the privacy of your own home, and to give your subconscious mind helpful posthypnotic suggestions.

These suggestions will include one to trigger the sub-conscious mind to activate the subconscious feel. With this, you will get the coordinated, rhythmic approach desired and needed for good bowling.

During hypnosis you will also mentally practice the correct bowling delivery by the use of visual imagery to more deeply impress the correct movements upon the subconscious memory.

Additionally, you will learn about time distortion under hypnosis, in which normal time is compressed and hours of mental practice can be accomplished in minutes.

YOU NEED HAVE NO FEARS

Hypnosis, as stated, is a recognized phenomenon. If you accept this statement, you have met the only requirement necessary to induce hypnosis.

A comfortable chair, a quiet and not-too-brightly lighted room, and the assurance of being undisturbed is all that is needed for the environment. Actually, you will find being in bed most satisfactory. It has the added advantage that at the completion of self-hypnosis you can drop right off to sleep.

Don't be afraid of inducing self-hypnosis. As Dr. Dorcus stated, "A hypnotized person won't do anything unless he wants to and won't stay in a trance if he wants to come out of it." The feeling you have as you enter the first stage of hypnosis may be compared to the moment before you drop off to sleep. If you wished, by sheer will power, you could rouse yourself and refuse to sleep. We are assuming, of course, that you really wish to be hypnotized.

The directions you give yourself need not be spoken

aloud nor need they be given by rote. The words used in the following instructions are given only as one example of how to induce self-hypnosis. You should use words that are familiar to you and give yourself suggestions that will help your individual game.

HERE'S HOW YOU START

Induce self-hypnosis as follows: Turn the lights out, lie down in a comfortable position on the bed and close your eyes. Say to yourself:

"I am now going to relax every muscle in my body ... starting from my feet ... and going to my head ... The toes on my right foot are relaxing ... They feel limp ... limp ... heavy and relaxed ... This relaxation is creeping up through the ball and the arch of my foot ... all the way to my ankle ... so that my right foot is completely relaxed . . . relaxed and heavy . . . heavy and limp . . . Now the toes on my left foot are relaxing in the same way ... First my toes ... limp and heavy ... Now my left arch and heel ... heavy and relaxed ... heavy and limp ... My left foot is completely relaxed ... relaxed and limp ... My left foot is completely relaxed ... Both feet are now completely relaxed ... completely relaxed ... relaxed and heavy ... This heaviness is creeping up the calf of my right leg ... so that I am now completely relaxed from the tip of my right toes to my knee ... Now my left calf is relaxing in the same manner ... Both of my feet and legs are completely relaxed up to my knees ... This relaxation is extending up through the large muscles of my right thigh ... so that my right leg is completely relaxed up to my hip ... Now I am letting my left thigh also relax ... so that both of my feet and legs

81

are heavy . . . heavy and relaxed . . . heavy and relaxed . . . relaxed and limp . . . so relaxed . . . so limp . . . Now the fingers on my right hand are relaxing . . . They are getting limp and heavy . . . and relaxed . . . I feel my right hand relaxing more and more . . . getting more and more limp . . . more and more heavy . . . Now the fingers of my left hand are letting go completely . . . All the muscles are relaxing . . . My fingers are getting heavy . . . limp . . . relaxed . . . My left hand is now completely relaxed and heavy . . . This feeling is now flowing up my arms . . . My right forearm is relaxed and heavy . . . My left forearm limp and heavy . . . My right upper arm is relaxed . . . heavy . . . heavy . . . My left upper arm is relaxed . . . relaxed and limp . . . Both of my hands and arms are completely relaxed . . . relaxed and heavy . . . heavy and limp . . . Now I am going to relax my body . . . My hips . . . back muscles . . . abdomen . . . chest muscles . . . shoulders . . . will all relax at the same time . . . I shall take a deep breath . . . hold it . . . and release it slowly . . . My entire body is relaxing . . . I am breathing deeply . . . and slowly . . . My body is now completely relaxed . . . I feel pleasantly limp and heavy . . . relaxed and limp . . . My body is completely relaxed . . . and I am breathing slowly . . . evenly . . . The muscles in my neck are now beginning to relax . . . My head is becoming so heavy . . . All the muscles in my face are limp . . . relaxed and loose . . . From my neck to the top of my head I am completely relaxed . . . I feel pleasantly free from tension . . . Every muscle and every nerve in my entire body is completely relaxed . . . My body feels loose . . . and heavy . . . completely relaxed . . . My body is resting calmly . . . I am fully at ease . . . Every muscle . . . every nerve . . . in my entire body . . . is completely relaxed . . ."

HERE'S THE HYPNOTIC TECHNIQUE

It is very important to relax your body thoroughly before continuing with self-hypnosis. Should you have trouble relaxing any part of your body, you can make it release all its tension by concentrating upon it individually. After each instruction you give yourself, be sure to pause until it works. Do not will your body to relax. This only brings the conscious mind into play and defeats your purpose. When you have attained this feeling of relaxation over your entire body, open your eyes.

Select an object above eye level, so that there is a slight strain on the eyes and eyelids. A bit of light reflection, a picture frame, or where the wall joins the ceiling does nicely for a focal point. At this time you try to get your eyelids to close at a specific count such as the count of three. This could just as well be a count of ten, twenty, or one hundred. Actually you are trying to establish a conditioned response to a specific count. When you have an irresistible urge to close your eyes on or before you reach the completion of the count, you know that you are in a heightened state of suggestibility or self-hypnosis. This is the first test for determining if you have achieved self-hypnosis. You do not rush the count, but try to consciously create a heavy, watery feeling which you again purposely intensify by self-suggestion as you continue counting until such time that you close your eyes because it becomes uncomfortable to keep them open. You may accomplish this readily or it may take you five, ten, or fifteen minutes. Whatever time is necessary initially to accomplish this will be decreased as you condition yourself every night.

Let us suppose that you try to get an eye closure but

the test doesn't work. You either are not taking enough time to first relax, you are not in the right psychological frame of mind or the conditioning process hasn't yet been established sufficiently. If this is the case, take more time to achieve a good state of relaxation and adopt the attitude that you are entering into a very beneficial and pleasurable state. Lastly, if your eyes do not close involuntarily, close them voluntarily and follow through with the desired post-hypnotic suggestions *as though you were in the hypnotic state.* The last statement is very important because as you do this, the conditioned response pattern will be established and you will achieve the positive results that you desire.

THE EYE CLOSURE TEST

Here are suggestions that you can use to accomplish the eye test. Remember, do not memorize the exact words; just the form is important. The following suggestions should be correlated with your psychological as well as physical reactions:

"As I complete the count of ten, my eyelids will become very heavy, watery, and tired. Even before I complete the count of ten, it may become necessary for me to close my eyes. The moment I do, I shall fall into a state of self-hypnosis. I shall be fully conscious, hear everything, and be able to direct suggestions to my subconscious mind. *One* . . . my eyelids are becoming very heavy . . . *Two* . . . My eyelids are becoming very watery . . . *Three* . . . My eyelids are becoming very tired . . . *Four* . . . I can hardly keep my eyes open . . . *Five* . . . I am beginning to close my eyes . . . *Six* . . . My eyelids are closing more and more . . . *Seven* . . . I am completely relaxed and at ease . . . *Eight* . . . It is becoming impossible for me to keep my eyelids open ... *Nine* ... It is impossible for me to keep my eyelids open ... *Ten* ... My eyes are closed, I am in the self-hypnotic state, and I can give myself whatever post-hypnotic suggestions I desire."

At this point, using the visual imagery technique, you mentally picture the good bowler that you want to be. You visualize yourself playing with perfect form and in an easy and relaxed manner. You might feel a bit uneasy about giving yourself these suggestions, but do it! It's your key to better bowling.

THE SWALLOWING TEST

Here is another test you can use to determine if you have achieved self-hypnosis. You can give yourself this test directly after your period of relaxation or following the eye closure test. This test is known as the swallowing test. Here are the suggestions you can use:

"As I count to ten and even before I reach the count of ten, I shall get an irresistable urge to swallow one time. As soon as I swallow one time, this feeling will leave me and I'll feel normal again in every respect. *One* ... My lips are dry ... *Two* .. My throat is becoming dry ... *Three* ... I am beginning to get an urge to swallow ... *Four* ... This urge is becoming stronger ... *Five* ... My throat feels parched ... *Six* ... The urge to swallow is becoming stronger and stronger ... *Seven* ... I feel an involuntary urge to swallow ... *Eight* ... This involuntary urge is becoming stronger and stronger ... *Nine* ... I must swallow ... *Ten* ... I have swallowed one time and am now in a self-hypnotic state in which I am very receptive to positive suggestions."

With this test you wait until you swallow without

conscious direction. When you do, you know you have achieved a state of heightened suggestibility. The act of swallowing has been directed and controlled by your subconscious mind as ordered by your conscious mind. After the swallowing test is successfully completed, you can give yourself whatever suggestions you want pertaining to your bowling.

THE HAND TEST

Here is a third test you can use for determining your receptivity to suggestions. You use the same general pattern that you did for the eye closure test and swallowing test. Remember, these suggestions should not be memorized verbatim; just the form is important.

"As I count ten and even before I reach the count of ten, I shall experience a tingling, light, or numb feeling in my right hand ... *One* ... I am concentrating upon my right hand ... As I think of it, picture it ... completely relaxed ... *Two* ... I shall feel a pleasant ... tingling ... sensation ... in my hand ... *Three* ... In my mind ... I see my right hand ... It is limp ... and heavy ... very relaxed ... *Four* ... I am completely at ease ... *Five* ... My hand is beginning to tingle ... *Six* ... It is a very pleasant sensation ... relaxed ... tingling ... *Seven* ... It is becoming stronger and stronger ... *Eight* ... It is a very pleasant feeling ... *Nine* ... I can feel a very pleasant, tingling feeling ... *Ten* ... I am now in a state of self-hypnosis and can give myself beneficial post-hypnotic suggestion especially pertaining to bowling ..."

If your subconscious mind has taken over, you will find your right hand has a tingling sensation in it. *You must remember* after any test with body action, a direction must be given to have it return to normal. Otherwise, the light, tingling sensation could continue after the completion of hypnosis. Now you say:

"The sensation in my hand will go away; it will return to normal ... I now have proof ... that I have reached a state of hypnosis ... Every muscle ... and nerve ... in my entire body ... is completely relaxed ... I feel wonderfully well ... I shall now give constructive instructions to my subconscious mind ... in order to improve my bowling ..."

GET A CLEAR PICTURE OF WHAT YOU WANT

At this point you may start giving yourself specific suggestions for improving your bowling. These suggestions should be carefully planned before induction so you will know what to tell your subconscious mind. Give the mental pictures and suggestions to yourself positively so as to remove the need for examination or challenge by the conscious mind. All you are seeking to do in self-hypnosis is to distract your conscious mind, thus eliminating the power of reasoning.

Picture yourself making a smooth, coordinated bowling delivery. Repeat this mental delivery until you are convinced it would not be made in any other way. Remember it is this subconscious feel recorded in your subconscious memory that is being sought so that it may be activated during actual practice and competition.

"But I don't know how I look bowling. How can I see myself making the delivery?" you ask.

Picture yourself as you would like to look. Picture yourself in the place of a professional you have admired for his smooth delivery while on television. You need not worry about copying his style, so long as you do not pick out any peculiarities of his form. What you are looking for is rhythm and coordination.

Too much cannot be said concerning the subconscious feel. You will know what it is to have confidence in your game once you know this feeling of "rightness." You will be able to bowl without stress or strain. Unless the subconscious feel has been deeply implanted so that the subconscious mind can deliver the ball automatically, distracting the conscious mind is useless. You would be by-passing your conscious mind without having established a subconscious pattern to direct the muscle movements.

Once you have received the sensation of the subconscious feel, even though it lasts only through a few frames, you will realize how important it is to reactivate it in order to attain the automatic delivery.

POSTHYPNOTIC SUGGESTIONS

Any directions given to the subconscious mind will be carried out unless countermanded during hypnosis. These directions are known as post-hypnotic suggestions which you give to yourself to be executed after you have terminated the hypnotic state. They may be effective for months and even years after the original post-hypnotic suggestion was given.

When you have finished implanting suggestions for better bowling in your subconscious mind, you should give yourself a post-hypnotic suggestion that the next time you practice self-hypnosis you will enter a deeper state more quickly. This is the technique used by hypnotists to facilitate hypnosis in the same subject the next time. Say to yourself:

"The next time I hypnotize myself . . . I shall fall into

a deeper . . . and more relaxed state . . . I will be able to relax my body more quickly . . . and easily . . . The next time I bowl . . . my body will be relaxed . . . and my mind will be at ease . . . The subconscious feel I have just experienced . . . will be brought into play . . . and my game will improve . . . I know these positive suggestions will work for me . . . At the count of three . . . I will open my eyes . . . I will be completely relaxed . . . and at ease . . . At the count of three . . . I will feel wonderfully refreshed . . . I will feel wide awake . . . and full of renewed energy . . . At the count of three . . . I will open my eyes . . . and feel completely relaxed . . . *One* . . . Every muscle . . . every nerve . . . in my entire body is completely relaxed . . . I feel wonderfully relaxed . . . *Two* . . . Every muscle . . . every nerve . . . in my entire body is relaxed . . . and rested . . . I feel wonderfully well . . . completely relaxed . . . *Three* . . . My eyes are open . . . and I feel wonderfully refreshed . . . completely relaxed . . ."

The three tests you have been given for proof of self-hypnosis are sufficient. Additional tests are not needed. You will find that after you have practiced self-hypnosis for a short period these tests will no longer be necessary because you will recognize instantly when you are in a hypnotic state.

You must remember that even though you feel you may not have achieved hypnosis (which is common), the suggestions you give yourself must, of necessity, spill over into your subconscious mind. This means the suggestions will work for you even though you do not feel as you anticipated.

Why is it so difficult to believe you are in a hypnotic state? Because you do not feel any appreciable difference from your normal waking state. You are probably looking for something to happen. Since you don't know what this "something" is, you are positive you are not hypnotized because you are aware of everything that is going on. You are not knocked out, and, because of this, you reason you are not under hypnosis.

The easiest way to recognize if you have reached the hypnotic state is to give yourself the three tests: eye closure, swallowing, and hand tingling. If you achieve only one of these tests, the others will come through practice. If you achieve none, then take a longer count. You can count to 100 if you need this period of time to assure eye closure. The closing of the eyes is the first sign that you are in a receptive frame of mind. Regardless of the depth that you have achieved, and whether or not you have responded to any of the tests, *you should always give yourself whatever suggestions you desire as though you were in a very deep state of hypnosis.* "But," you ask, "if I'm not under hypnosis, why give myself the suggestions?" You do this so that you will begin to form the conditioned reflex pattern.

Should you fall asleep while working with self-hypnosis, it is perfectly all right. The suggestions will reach the subconscious while you are passing from consciousness to sleep.

Some may achieve self-hypnosis almost instantly; others will succeed only after many weeks of practice. Much depends upon how seriously you practice the techniques explained in this book.

THE IMPORTANT THING TO KEEP IN MIND IS THAT IF YOU PERSEVERE YOU WILL FINALLY ACQUIRE THE CONDITIONED REFLEX PATTERN WHICH IS THE BASIS OF SELF-HYPNOSIS. THIS

WILL IMPROVE YOUR BOWLING IMMEASUR-ABLY. KEEP AT IT!

Chapter 9

Better Bowling Through Mental Pictures

GET THE PICTURE RIGHT

The secret of good bowling is the player's ability to summon up visual images or mental pictures. It is like watching oneself following a taped television performance.

There are two mental pictures used to improve bowling. One is the visual image of the delivery; the other is the roll of the ball to the pins.

You must get a clear picture in your mind of what your body is doing during the delivery. Picture yourself in balance as you take the stance, with a straight, smooth approach to the foul line, a pendulum-like arm movement close to the body, a coordinated slide and an easy lift and release. Actually see your thumb come out of the ball first so that the fingers give the lift for the spin to impart the hook.

This is like punching the correct data on an IBM machine. Unless it is fed in correctly, you can't get the correct answer. The subconscious mind can respond only with the memory pattern it has been given. Unless it has the correct movements in the memory, it is unable to direct the nerves and muscles to perform them.

Dr. Maxwell Maltz, in his recent book, *Psycho-Cybernetics,* which was condensed by *Reader's Digest* under the title, "Your Built-in Success Mechanism," says, "Though infinitely more complex, the human subconscious and nervous system bear a startling resemblance to that man-made marvel, the electronic brain. They appear to operate on the same general principles."

In discussing cybernetics (from the Greek word meaning steersman), which is the science of studying machines and mechanical principles for the purpose of reaching a particular goal, Dr. Maltz says, "It sees the so-called subconscious mind as not a mind at all but a mechanism—a goal-striving servo-mechanism consisting of the brain and nervous system which is used and directed by the mind.

"This mechanism within us is impersonal and automatic; like any other servo-mechanism it makes use of stored information or memory and it works on the data we feed into it." You will recognize this as a technical way of explaining exactly what we have been saying on the mechanism of the subconscious mind.

THE AUTOMATIC RESPONSE

The subconscious mind must be trained, educated, or, more correctly, given the thought pattern to execute the muscle direction through practice. When this is thoroughly accomplished, it then becomes simply an act of triggering the subconscious, as when the IBM operator punches a key, to obtain the previously recorded information.

An example of a thoroughly trained subconscious mind is that of an expert typist, whose fingers fly over the keys of a typewriter. The conscious mind triggers the response with words or complete thoughts. The subconscious mind reacts by directing the individual finger movements to strike the keys for the letters of the words.

The beginning typist, however, falters at the keyboard. Without proper training, the subconscious mind is unable to supply the automatic response. It calls upon the conscious mind for help. The conscious mind must then divert its attention to the finger movements on the keyboard.

This subconscious response is identical in all automatic movements. The inexperienced driver is forced to divert his conscious attention from maneuvering the car through traffic to directing the mechanical movements of his hands and feet to operate the mechanisms of the automobile.

The expert bowler, like the expert typist and driver, is able to focus his attention upon the pin set and the subconscious directs all the mechanical movements of the delivery of the ball. If there is a breakdown of the subconscious memory pattern, the conscious mind is forced to redirect the muscles. Timing and rhythm are destroyed, just as they are for the inexperienced typist or driver.

THE MENTAL PICTURE FOR LEARNING

"Is it possible to learn a physical action from just picturing it mentally?" you ask. "Don't the muscles have to move to be trained?"

Muscles respond to commands from the mind through the nervous system. To build strength into them, they must be exercised. But to train them, you train the mind which delivers the commands they obey.

Research Quarterly recently reported an experiment on the effect of mental practice in the physical movements of tossing a basketball through a hoop. Two groups of college students were given a 20-day test. One group actually practiced throwing the ball for a period every day. On the 20th day, scoring was improved 24 percent. The other students spent 20 minutes a day imagining they were throwing the ball at the basket. Their scoring improved 23 percent. Amazingly, only one percent difference appeared between those throwing and those using mental imagery.

The United States army conducted an experiment using visual imagery with 75 arm-and-hand amputee patients. Under hypnosis, they were given subordinate handwriting (left hand for right-handed persons and vice versa) instruction. The patients saw themselves writing with the hand they normally did not use. The results using this method more than doubled the expectancy.

But the point to be remembered is that the mental picture must be correct. The subconscious mind reacts exactly to the information it receives. You must give it the mental picture of how you wish to look while you are bowling.

HYPNOSIS IS QUICKER

"But why under hypnosis?" you ask. "What difference would there be if I just sat down and tried to form a mental picture of myself using good bowling form?"

The conscious mind is in a constant state of flux. It is impossible to hold to a single thought for more than a moment or two. Try it and see how long you can think of just one thing before something else pops into your mind. It is also constantly aware of all outside distractions. That is why concentration is so difficult.

Under self-hypnosis, with the body completely relaxed, outside distractions and awareness are cut to a minimum and a more positive picture of what you wish to give the subconscious mind can be made. Remember, the subconscious mind is like a recording device. The deeper the impression is implanted, the more readily it can be recalled.

J. Louis Orton, the noted British authority on hypnotism, states: "Self-hypnosis consists of the deliberate employment of mental pictures to influence oneself."

Writing on visual imagery, Dr. S. J. Van Pelt, president of the British Society of Medical Hypnotists, declares: "This writer has found the visual technique to be one of great value. The patient is instructed, while under only light hypnosis, to picture himself acting and looking the way he wants to act and look. In the normal state, he retains the memory and performs the role."

Under self-hypnosis, go over your bowling time and time again. See yourself until you have the feeling that although you are lying still, you are actually making the smooth, balanced delivery. When this becomes deeply enough implanted in the subconscious memory, you need only trigger the subconscious feel for the response of the automatic movements.

PICTURE THE PERFECT STRIKE

The second visual image is the roll of the ball from the time of release until it reaches the pin set. This is what the experts like Ed Lubanski have in mind when they say, "Just look to spilling the pins."

Subconscious response comes from positive conscious demands upon it. A negative thought produces a negative result. James Bender, in his book, *Victory Over Fear,* states: "The body never acts, it only reacts. This is why the fearful person is tense. The negative ideas he concentrates on are translated into negative bodily reactions."

Negative thinking can limit your ability, if you let it. And, conversely, you have the power to think positively to increase your ability. Memories of past failures may adversely affect your present performance, if you dwell on them. "I missed that split before, so I'll probably miss it again," you say. But if you dismiss such thoughts of failure from your mind and picture how the ball can be rolled to convert the remaining pins for a spare, saying to yourself, "It can be made and I can make it," you have a good chance to succeed.

The subconscious mind retains all memories, both of success and failure. Call upon it for the memory of success so that it can direct the muscle action that resulted in success. As you know, a positive attitude is invaluable in anything that we endeavor to do.

Conscious concern and fear in any action create tension. Confidence is the only antidote for the poison of fear. Confidence is gained by calling upon the memory of success, rather than failure.

A mental picture of the ball rolling down the lane to strike the pin set at the point to produce results will activate the subconscious feel for the muscle movements necessary to produce this end result.

THE ONLY EFFECTIVE WAY TO EMPLOY THE POWER OF MENTAL PICTURES IS TO COMMIT THEM TO YOUR SUBCONSCIOUS MIND DURING HYPNOSIS. WHEN THIS IS DONE, THEY ARE NO LONGER VISUAL IMAGES. THEY ARE TRANSFORMED AND RECORDED AS SUBCONSCIOUS

FEEL WHICH CAN BE INSTANTANEOUSLY ACTI-
VATED BY A THOUGHT FROM THE CONSCIOUS
MIND.

Chapter 10

Seven Hours Practice In Seven Minutes

TIME DISTORTION UNDER HYPNOSIS

The subconscious mind does not record the passage of time the same way as the conscious mind.

The conscious mind records time physically, by means of a clock. It is objective and tells you that a thought or movement requires a certain number of seconds, minutes, hours, or days.

Your subconscious mind has an entirely different concept of time that has nothing to do with the physical world. It is called subjective because your own sense of the passage of time is used.

Personal time varies according to the circumstances in which you find yourself. Haven't you noticed that when you are happy or extremely interested in something, time passes quickly? On the other hand, if you are sad or anxious, time seems to drag.

This is called time distortion. When you continue in a happy state, time is automatically shortened. When you are in a state of unhappiness, pain or anxiety, time automatically lengthens. This explains why a drowning man can review his entire life within seconds. Psychologists know this is possible, because your subconscious mind contains a complete record of everything that has happened to you since birth. Therefore, in moments of extreme distress your subconscious has the ability to distort and manipulate time.

If you have ever encountered· danger or had a narrow escape, you probably experienced time distortion. Everything about you went into slow motion, and time seemed to stand still until the action was over. At that point, objective time started up again and everything returned to normal.

We have mentioned previously that it always seems shorter on the way back than it does going? The reason for this is that on the way to a place the conscious mind is alert to directions. On the way back, the subconscious knows the way and the conscious mind is occupied with other things. Therefore, subjectively speaking, the time involved in returning would seem shorter. Albert Einstein said that subjective time is not measurable.

Another example of time distortion happens when you dream. A dream which seemingly goes on for hours is actually experienced in a few seconds or minutes by the clock.

The theory of "sleep learning" is derived from this fact. Ramon Vinay, the talented Metropolitan opera star, used it to great advantage when he accepted a role to sing opposite Kirsten Flagstad in *Tristan*. Being unavoidably detained in Chile, he was unable to reach San Francisco in time for rehearsals. He memorized his role by sleeping with the speaker of an automatic record player under his pillow. The music was imbued so well in his subconscious mind that he was able to sing the role in a language he did not understand without missing a single cue. With only two piano rehearsals and one rehearsal with the orchestra, he sang so well that opera critic Alfred Frankenstein wrote: "He brought a tenderness, lyricism and fragility of expression that were altogether unprecedented."

MOTION PICTURE STARS HAVE LEARNED THIS SECRET

Time sense can be deliberately altered by hypnotic suggestion. Employing time distortion under hypnosis, it is possible to imbue the subconscious mind with thought patterns in an inconceivably short period. Thus, it is possible to condense seven hours of bowling practice into seven minutes.

Many motion picture and television stars are using hypnosis to assist them in quickly learning their lines. Some use self-hypnosis, while others employ professional hypnotists to assist them. The results are the same, for if you learn self-hypnosis you can produce the same effect as a hypnotist. The power of hypnosis is the power of belief. If you accept a suggestion from yourself and are convinced that it will be helpful it has the same power as the hypnotist's words.

Actress Linda Darnell accepted her first stage role in the play, "Late Love," and became emotionally disturbed because she did not have time to learn her lines before the play was scheduled to open. Her Beverly Hills physician flew to Chicago and placed Miss Darnell in a hypnotic state and had the lines for her part read to her.

Scoring a smash hit in the play, Miss Darnell said after her first performance, "I never felt so secure about playing a role in my life. Hypnosis not only made it possible for me to remember the lines, but helped me feel the part completely."

Dr. Ivar Birkeland of Seattle, Washington, reported an experiment in which he said he reduced a patient's golf score by 15 strokes after a single session of hypnosis.

IT BECOMES EVEN EASIER

You, too, can use hypnosis with time distortion to practice and improve your bowling. Before you hypnotize yourself, carefully study sequence pictures of the correct basic movements of the bowling delivery. Place yourself in the positions so that you can memorize the movements of the hands, arms, shoulders, hips, legs and feet.

Examine them until you can close your eyes and see yourself making the delivery. If you have any questions about the mechanical movements, check them with the instructor at your local bowling lanes. The conscious mind must have no doubts when it instructs the subconscious mind during hypnosis. Any doubts will be recorded, so be sure to give the mental picture to your subconscious in a positive manner.

Make the delivery in slow motion. See every movement. Watch yourself in the pushaway, the pendulum-like arm swing and the slide. See your thumb come out of the ball to produce the lift and spin.

After visualizing yourself in slow motion, speed it up. See yourself making the delivery as you would at the lanes. This will produce the subconscious feel that you will call on when you are actually bowling.

Frequent visualization of your bowling under hypnosis will make the scenes become more real. With each mental practice session, there will be an increase in detail and color. Your thought processes will seem similar to those in the normal waking state. They will be much more helpful, however, because under hypnosis you can consider your game as a whole, without outside distractions.

THERE'S PLENTY OF TIME

When you use time distortion during hypnosis, you should tell yourself that there is no hurry. You have all the time you need to review as many deliveries as you like. This is true because the number of deliveries that can be made in a matter of minutes under hypnosis would require hours at the bowling lane in practice.

Activity that seems to proceed at a normal or natural rate will actually take place with great rapidity when you are hypnotized. For example, among hundreds of experiments conducted by Dr. Linn F. Cooper and Dr. Milton H. Erickson and reported in their book, *Time Distortion in Hypnosis,* page 81, a subject was asked to review, under hypnosis, a basketball game he had witnessed. "The subject was able to see the entire game in the interval between two handclaps as close together as the experimenter could space them," the report claimed.

REMEMBER, EVEN THOUGH YOU REMAIN MOTIONLESS THROUGHOUT HYPNOSIS, YOU ARE PRACTICING YOUR PHYSICAL GAME BY TRAINING YOUR SUBCONSCIOUS MEMORY. BY UTILIZING TIME DISTORTION, YOU WILL RECEIVE THE BENEFIT OF MANY HOURS OF PRACTICE AT THE BOWLING LANE IN A RELATIVELY SHORT PERIOD OF MENTAL PRACTICE.

Chapter 11

Pin, Spot Or Line . . . It's Concentration

HERE'S THE FINAL SECRET TO GOOD BOWLING

While bowling allows great diversity in style and technique, probably the most controversial aspect involves the target used to line up the delivery. There are three methods, pin, spot and line, each top bowling star claiming one of these to be the best suited for him.

Pin bowlers follow the theory that since the bowler is aiming to knock down the pins, he should aim at the target—the pins.

The theory of the spot bowlers is that instead of aiming at the pins which are 60 feet away, you aim at a closer target—a spot on the lane. It may be the "range finders" which are spots stamped into the bed of the lane 12 to 16 feet beyond the foul line or a particular spot you may choose by looking at the maple boards.

The line bowlers combine both techniques to form an imaginary line leading from a spot into the 1-3 pocket.

They first concentrate upon the spot and do not take their eyes off it until the ball has rolled past it.

This controversy over line, spot or pin is probably the most discussed single phase of the bowling delivery. "With three different targets, how can all work equally well?" you ask.

The answer, once you appreciate it, is amazingly simple —and it provides the final secret to good bowling.

The target is selected at the time you take your stance. It then becomes a matter of footwork to approach the foul line in a straight line for the slide and release.

THE TARGET—PIN, SPOT OR LINE—IS UNIMPORTANT EXCEPT AS A FOCAL POINT FOR YOUR SUBCONSCIOUS DELIVERY OF THE BALL.

THE SUBCONSCIOUS FEEL MAKES THE DELIVERY

"What?" you exclaim. "Do you mean to say I don't need to pick out a target? How am I going to know at what point to make the release?"

No, that wasn't what was said. The target is important to line up your delivery, like taking aim with a rifle, to bring your body to the foul line in a position to release the ball. But it is unimportant what target you select, so long as you allow your subconscious mind to direct the muscle action in order to reach a position at the foul line so that the ball can be delivered along the path to the 1-3 pocket.

What is important is to concentrate your conscious attention upon whatever target you have selected. This then becomes the single object or thought that distracts the conscious mind from any interference with the subconscious delivery. It is like the whirling disc or crystal ball of the hypnotist or the reflected light or object you selected for self-hypnosis in order to concentrate the conscious attention.

In golf, the player concentrates his conscious attention upon the ball to distract his conscious mind from any interference in the stroke. In bowling, it is the pin, spot or line that serves this purpose.

This is the triggering device to activate the subconscious feel. It turns over to the subconscious mind the entire job of directing the muscle actions for which it has been trained during practice.

WITHOUT CONSCIOUS INTERFERENCE, THE SUBCONSCIOUS WILL PERFORM THE DUTIES EXACTLY AS IT DID DURING PRACTICE AND YOU CAN TAKE YOUR PRACTICE GAME WITH YOU INTO LEAGUE PLAY OR COMPETITION.

ACTIVATING THE SUBCONSCIOUS FEEL

Have you ever noticed a baseball player swinging his bat with short strokes as he waits for the pitcher to deliver the ball? Or a golfer waggling his club above the ball before a stroke? Possibly you have thought of these actions as meaningless or meant to loosen up the muscles or relieve nervous tension. They are far from meaningless. The players are activating the subconscious feel. They are actually mentally reviewing the swing or stroke that is about to be played.

Have you ever pounded a nail, giving it a couple of short taps before applying a full swing of the hammer, just to get the feel of it? What it amounts to is a miniature performance by the conscious mind to be certain that the subconscious is capable of responding with the correct muscle direction.

Good bowlers use this technique. You have seen them as they shuffle their feet to line up their bodies for the target. They seem to be weighing the ball in their hands, as they look down the approach to the foul line and then to the pins. Some bowlers make their delivery quickly while others take considerable time with their waggle. It depends upon how long it takes to activate the subconscious feel for the action.

Remember Joe Falcaro's warning about tension. "The ball seems to get heavier and more difficult to release." Without the subconscious feel the conscious mind becomes concerned whether the subconscious will be capable of the automatic response. It begins to redirect muscle movement and the muscles work against each other to produce tension.

If you have properly trained your subconscious mind through practice, activating the subconscious feel is easy. Hefting the ball while quickly reviewing what you wish to accomplish as you take your stance will trigger the subconscious to respond and deliver exactly as it was trained.

YOU CAN'T FAIL

If you can deliver a ball with a smooth, coordinated rhythm during practice, you can do the same thing in competition or league play if you concentrate your conscious attention upon the pins, spot or line.

AFTER YOU HAVE LEARNED THE BASIC DELIVERY THROUGH PRACTICE, NOTHING YOU CAN DO IS MORE IMPORTANT THAN TO COMPLETELY CONCENTRATE YOUR CONSCIOUS

ATTENTION UPON THE SPOT, PINS OR LINE
AFTER YOU HAVE TAKEN YOUR STANCE.

The only thing that can spoil your delivery is conscious
interference. And, as you have learned, the conscious
mind will interfere and produce tension whenever a
penalty is involved in an action. As the demonstration of
walking a plank showed, no amount of will power can
prevent this from happening.

It cannot be repeated too often that the only way of
eliminating tension when a penalty is involved (in the
case of bowling the failure to score well) is to distract
the conscious mind so that it is unaware that a penalty is
involved in the action. With complete concentration upon
the spot, pins or line, the conscious mind is distracted
from the thought of failure or penalty and the delivery
can be made subconsciously and automatically.

You cannot fail using this technique of hypnosis if the
subconscious memory pattern has been firmly established
with the correct automatic movements.

IF THERE'S STRAIN, YOU HAVEN'T GOT IT

"How can I tell whether or not I have activated the subconscious feel and am delivering the ball with subconscious control?" you ask.

If there is any feeling of strain or discomfort during
the delivery, you will know the movements have not become automatic. You can recognize the subconscious feel
by comparing your feelings with those experienced in
your good practice session. Actually, it is a lack of feeling.

You cannot develop the subconscious feel during competition or league play. Until you have learned how to
activate the subconscious feel and concentrate your con-

scious attention during practice, it is impossible to distract the conscious mind during the stress of competition. This accounts for the fact that some bowlers may play in several leagues each week, without showing any marked improvement. It is also the reason why the bowling stars put in as many as 50 or 60 practice games each week, in addition to their regular play.

At the beginning, you may find that you are able to bowl only a few frames with the subconscious feel before it deserts you. No matter how hard you try, the strain creeps back into your delivery. Remember, it isn't something you can consciously will. It can come only through concentration and practice.

THE YARDSTICK OF TENSION

"But what I can't understand," you say, "is why a one pin tap or missing a split gets me so shook up when it doesn't seem to bother other fellows."

Each person carries his own yardstick to measure his personal fears and anxieties. What may appear to be an insignificant problem for one person may seem insurmountable to another. Actually, the inexperienced low scorer has a bigger problem than the one who has learned to score well. It is a matter of confidence. The experienced player gets a difficult split and feels certain he can convert it into a spare. The inexperienced player can only think of how easily it can be missed for an open frame.

PRACTICE WILL GIVE YOU CONFIDENCE. WHEN YOU LEARN TO ACTIVATE THE SUBCONSCIOUS FEEL AND RELY UPON THE AUTOMATIC DELIVERY WHILE CONCENTRATING YOUR CONSCIOUS ATTENTION ON THE SPOT,

PINS OR LINE—YOU WILL HAVE LEARNED THE ENTIRE SECRET OF BECOMING A GOOD BOWLER.

Chapter 12

A Mark In Every Frame

IT'S THE SPARES THAT MAKE A GOOD BOWLER

Up to this point, we have talked about the bowling delivery to make a strike. This is the ultimate goal. With 12 strikes in a row, you have the perfect 300 game. And if it could be had easily, there would be little challenge or interest in bowling.

The mental problem remains constant and the physical delivery, except for a change in the angle of the attack, depending on which side of the lane the pins have been left, is identical for making spares or strikes.

But it is the ability to make the spares that gives a bowler a high average. With just a spare in every frame you could have a 190 average. And, conversely, it is possible to roll 9 strikes and come out with only a 129 game. A bowler of record managed this by shooting strike, strike, miss, strike, strike, miss, strike, strike, strike. He had a one-pin count in the 3, 6 and 9 frames.

There are some nearly impossible splits, such as the "Lily" (5-7-10). But one of the most frequently missed spares is the 10-pin tap.

The reason the experts miss the spares is because of increased tension. They can deliver the ball toward the 1-3 pocket automatically by concentrating their attention upon the spot, pins or line. But with the second ball, the blue chips are on the line. An open frame costs 10 points plus the pin count left standing. Fearful of a miss, they fail to roll the ball automatically and consciously try to steer it. Or, as Billy Golembiewski said: "I got too careful."

THE APPROACH ANGLE FOR SPARES

The less experienced bowler, in addition to freezing on the roll, may not know the right angle at which to attack the remaining pins to allow himself the least margin of error. For that reason, we have included what the experts agree to be the best position to roll the ball to pick up the most commonly left taps and splits.

Study the pictures. Store them in your memory as securely as you have your bowling delivery. The easiest way to do this is to visualize the pins by their numbers.

During hypnosis, visualize the ball rolling toward the spares along the line which will give you the best chance of cleaning the boards. Then, when you are faced with making any of these splits, you can activate your subconscious feel and allow the delivery to be as automatic as it is for going for the full set.

Pay particular attention during practice as to how you are lined up to come into the foul line for the delivery that may take your ball across the lane in either direction.

Note where you are concentrating your aim on the target of either the spot, pins or line. In competition rely on your practice delivery and allow the approach and release to be completely automatic.

THE BASIC BOWLING FORM

As pointed out earlier, bowling stars all have their own peculiarities of delivery. Few of these experts try to deliberately copy the style of another. Claude Patterson is satisfied with his high backswing and fast delivery, while Johnny King sticks with practically no backswing and a five-step delivery. None of them have tried to copy Carter's "crooked arm" or Campi's "wrong foot."

They have found it just doesn't pay. Patterson, in commenting on his form, said: "A few years ago I was trying to improve my game. Taking a page from my teammates' book, I deliberately slowed my ball down. The result was two years of comparatively poor bowling. It ruined my timing and footwork—in fact, it made me feel as if I was learning to bowl all over again."

But all of the bowling stars have a basic bowling form which gives them timing and coordination. Violating the basic form can only lead to unnatural movements which will set up tension in the delivery.

The basic bowling form is illustrated. Study it. Close your eyes and see yourself making the same movements. Compare it during practice with your own delivery.

If you find something radically different between your delivery and the basic form, analyze what it is and why you are doing it. Is it helping your game, or is it setting up tension by having the muscles work against each other?

Consistent bowling occurs only when delivery becomes automatic. You must depend on a conditioned reflex action to perform the identical movements repeatedly. Check your delivery often during practice to see that no stress or strain creeps in to prevent you from making the delivery automatic.

YOU'RE THE ONLY ONE WHO CAN DO IT

No therapy, theory or technique is of value unless you surrender yourself to it. No one can do your thinking for you. You are the only one who can give yourself the subconscious feel. You are the only one who can activate it. You are the only one who can concentrate your attention upon the spot, pins or line.

Self-hypnosis for better bowling remains only a theory until you put it into practice. A bridge, a building, a painting are all created in the mind, but they do not become realities until their creators translate their thoughts into actions.

You can't become a good bowler by wishing. You must spend time practicing . . . practicing . . . practicing. Self-hypnosis can help you. It will make your job much easier. But mastery comes through hard work. The champions remain champions because they practice constantly. The poor and average bowler becomes better through continued practice.

Frank Clause was a school teacher; Lou Campi, a brick mason. Ed Lubanski worked in a grocery store. The stars have come from all walks of life. They had one thing in common—the determination to master the sport of bowling. Not one of them had any more talent than you have —just the determination.

The mental side of bowling is the blue print; practice is the construction that develops it to a reality. The time required for both mental and physical play can be greatly reduced by using time distortion during hypnosis. However, the subconscious feel can only be found through practice. Your bowling will improve immeasurably now that you know the goal you are seeking in practice.

Talk about your new goals and aspirations with your friends. By repeating them, you will implant these ideas more deeply in your own mind. You will find they become clearer and more defined as you explain them. Speak of your goal with confidence. Know what you are going to do, how you are going to do it, then do it!

There will always be those who scoff at any new idea as being a gimmick. These scoffers are usually unwilling to spend the time and effort to examine and try a new idea. What they are actually looking for is some patented gimmick that will reward them with a better game without work or practice. There just isn't such a thing.

THE USE OF SELF-HYPNOSIS TO MASTER BOWLING IS NOT DIFFICULT; BUT IT IS NOT A GIFT. YOU MUST EARN IT THROUGH PRACTICE. CONSTANT REPETITION WILL MAKE IT MORE DIFFICULT FOR YOUR CONSCIOUS MIND TO INTERFERE AND CAUSE YOU TO LOSE THE SUBCONSCIOUS FEEL DURING COMPETITION. YOU WILL HAVE MASTERED BOWLING WHEN YOU CAN DELIVER EVERY BALL AUTOMATICALLY. THE PROOF WILL APPEAR ALONGSIDE YOUR NAME ON THE SCORE SHEET.

Chapter 13

Question And Answer Period

Perhaps the following questions and answers will help solve some problems that are bothering you about self-hypnosis or bowling.

Q: Are you certain there isn't something more to inducing self-hypnosis than the simple instructions you have given?

A: Absolutely certain. You may check other books if you like, but you will find the means of producing hypnosis are exactly the same.

Q: I talked about using self-hypnosis to improve my bowling with some friends. They said it's impossible. Is it?

A: The use of hypnosis in bowling represents a new application of this science. If your friends have not read this book, they cannot give you a valid opinion. If this book has made sense to you, why don't you try it and be your own judge?

Q: What is the difference between self-hypnosis and positive thinking? It seems to me they are the same thing.

A: The two terms are often confused as being the same. Positive thinking deals only with the conscious mind. This is just the first step in self-hypnosis. The second step is to transfer these positive thoughts from the conscious to the subconscious through the use of hypnosis. When applied to bowling, it produces the subconscious feel.

Q: If professional bowlers use self-hypnosis, why don't they say anything about it? Maybe you're twisting their words around to make it look like they do.

A: Many professionals unknowingly describe the application of self-hypnosis for bowling in different terms. Don't blame the pros if they don't recognize it by name. It has only been within the past few years that it has been recognized by the medical profession.

Q: I was so anxious to learn to bowl, I took lessons from an instructor. Until I learned about self-hypnosis, I didn't know what he was talking about when he tried to describe the mental side of bowling. I always thought it was just a physical act. Now we spend more time talking than we do bowling, and I'm coming along just fine. Is there any specific thing I should do in order to improve my game?

A: Go even further. Use time distortion and mental imagery when you practice. See if you don't come along even faster.

Q: Manipulation of time during hypnosis intrigues me. Where can I find more information about it?

A: One of the best books on the subject is *Time Distortion In Hypnosis* by Linn F. Cooper, M.D. and Milton H. Erickson, M.D.

Q: I tried self-hypnosis, but it isn't curing my exceptionally high backswing. I realize that this is a physical movement and doesn't concern the mental part of the game. Have you any suggestions to remedy this?

A: Yes. You know that all muscle movements, voluntary and involuntary, are controlled by your mind. Your high backswing is the result of conscious effort. Once you have discovered the subconscious feel, your backswing won't be so high. The best way to get this subconscious feel is to consciously study the movements of the experts. Watching television stars also would be a great help to you.

Q: You said that tensions produce unwanted muscular action. Do you have any actual proof of this?

A: Northrop Aviation researchers conducted scientific tests to determine the amount of muscle strain produced by tension in order to learn its effect upon astronauts for space travel.

Tiny electrodes were taped to the bodies of test pilots. The results were recorded upon a telemeter. When the pilots were placed in a simulated space ship and told they were to control it, the computer showed only a quarter of a degree drop in temperatures and moderate muscle tension.

Then they were told something had gone wrong, and they were in possible danger. Muscle tension increased four times and some temperatures dropped two degrees. The men were unable to react or perform with normal efficiency.

Q: I have been able to induce self-hypnosis, and it has worked wonders for my game. However, there are days when I am so keyed up, I just can't get it to work. When this happens, I go back to the way I used to bowl, which wasn't good. What can I do about it?

A: Even pros have days when personal or business problems are more pressing than bowling. When your conscious mind is filled with these problems, you will have difficulty concentrating upon your game. If you use self-hypnosis to help solve some of these other problems, it will give you more time for your bowling thoughts.

Q: I have a friend who says nobody can hypnotize him. Do you think he could be hypnotized?

A: I can't think of anyone who would want to hypnotize him against his wishes. Under the right conditions he can be hypnotized if he is motivated to be hypnotized. The only requirement is a willingness on his part.

Q: I have seen some of the big pros throw gutter balls. What happened to their mental game?

A: Men are human, not machines. Bowling is a game, not a test of physical fitness or endurance.

Pros make only one mistake at a time if they stay up in the money. It's the dub who lets one mistake disturb him so that he makes another. One open frame in a series won't hurt you if you don't follow it with a second or third.

Q: How can I tell if I am using my conscious or subconscious mind when I bowl?

A: Usually the score sheet will tell you if you are letting your conscious mind control the delivery. If you feel any strain or muscle tension, you can be sure your conscious mind has gotten into the act. The subconscious feel is almost effortless.

Q: I have heard it said that if you are hypnotized too many times, it will make your mind weak. Is this true?

A: In hypnosis you concentrate thoughts along constructive channels. Knowing how to concentrate will improve your mind and general mental attitude rather than weaken it.

Q: I am still puzzled about the subconscious feel. Can you describe it a little more fully for me?

A: If, when you dance, you let your feet react subconsciously to the rhythm of the music, you are experiencing the subconscious feel. If you try to consciously make certain steps as you do when you are learning to dance, the motions will be jerky. It is the subconscious feel that makes a good dancer. It is the same subconscious feel that will make you a good bowler.

Q: I am interested in learning more about self-hypnosis. Can you recommend a good book?

A: You might like to read *A Practical Guide to Self-Hypnosis* by Melvin Powers. In this book Mr. Powers not only thoroughly explains self-hypnosis but gives a thoughtful investigation into the reasons for its application.

Q: Has hypnosis been applied to sports other than bowling?

A: Yes. It has been used in sports as varied as golf, tennis, baseball, football, skiing, archery, swimming, basketball and track.

Dr. Huber Grimm, team physician of the Seattle University basketball team, recently related the results when Dave Mills, a six-foot five-inch, junior forward, asked for his help because he "froze" during competition. He had been benched on the eve of the West Coast Athletic Conference tournament in San Francisco. Spectators made Mills so fearful that he was afraid he would make mistakes—and in this frame of mind, of course, he did. Under hypnosis, Dr. Grimm suggested to Dave that he would be unaware of the spectators, completely relaxed and would play exceedingly well. Dr. Grimm asked coach Vince Cazzeta to allow Dave to play and the result was astounding. Mills scored 60 points and cleared 63 rebounds in a single game, and his brilliant play led to his selection on the all-tournament team.

"All I did was free his spirit," Dr. Grimm reported. "He was in need of confidence, and I gave it to him through hypnosis." The Associated Press told the story as follows: "Dave Mills, a vacuum cleaner off the backboards, led a fast-breaking Seattle University team to victory last night. It was hard to recognize Mills as the same player who has been with the Chieftans all year."

Dr. William S. Kroger, a pioneer in hypnosis, undertook to improve the batting of a professional baseball player with equally sensational results. The player had been "beaned," and his fear of a recurrence was so strong that he became "plate shy." He had changed his batting stance so that he always had "one foot in the bucket" so that he could back away from the plate more quickly. He was given a posthypnotic suggestion that such an event happening again was exceedingly remote, and this was amplified by suggestions of confidence that he would immediately start slugging as well as ever. His batting average soared immediately.

Dr. Michio Ikai, professor of physiology at Tokyo University, and Dr. Arthur H. Steinhaus of the George Williams College Laboratory of Physiology Research in Physical Education, Chicago, have proved that trackmen can far surpass their best previous times under hypnosis. Their tests, incidentally, proved that there is no danger of an athlete going beyond his physiologic limit while bettering his former marks. They attribute the superior performances to the removal of inhibitions which psychologically prevent an athlete from doing his best. This report was made before the International Congress on Health and Fitness in the Modern World held in Rome during the last Olympic games.

All reports, as a matter of fact, show that athletic performances are improved by psychological, not physical, means, and that built-in automatic reflexes protect the athlete against the danger of overexertion at all levels of awareness—hypnotic or nonhypnotic.

In conclusion, there is all the evidence needed that you can help your bowling game, as well as any other in which you wish to excel, through the use of hypnosis.

Q: Are there any bowling lanes where the hypnotic techniques described in this book are being used?

A: Yes. Melvin Powers, professional Los Angeles hypnotist, recently conducted an experiment with nine women bowlers in collaboration with Mort Katz, owner of the Citrus Bowl in San Fernando, California. The nine women—Marion Harmon, Deanie Robbins, Jeanne Wilcox, Shirley Killion, Rosalie Carr, Dorothy Gordon, Gloria Lang, Belle Katz and Cynthia Morse—all improved their games considerably, and enthusiastic letters concerning their experiences are on file. A typical story is that of Deanie Robbins who increased her average from 147 to 163 following employment of self-hypnosis. Dorothy Gordon raised her average from 135 to more than 150. Because of the successful results, Mr. Katz now teaches hypnosis to all his bowling students.

Sidney Newman, president of the Midtown Bowling Center in Los Angeles, is another bowling lane proprietor who is advancing the techniques described in this book.

He, too, reports that those who are conscientiously applying this method are dramatically improving their averages.

Q: Are there any professional bowlers using self-hypnosis?

A: Yes. The following article by Sam Levine appeared in the October 23, 1962 issue of *The Cleveland Kegler*.

Thompson Romps To City Match Title

Something has happened to Al Thompson.

And whatever it is, whether it is the music he hears when he sits on the bowler's bench, or the book on self-hypnosis *(How You Can Bowl Better Using Self-Hypnosis)* which he insists has helped his game, or the instructions he received from Buzz Fazio of Detroit, Thompson, today, throws a bowling ball as well as any kegler in the country.

And better than most of them.

Thompson made a shambles of the Men's All-Star Qualifier, which ended last Sunday night at Playhouse Square Bowling Center. He moved into first place after the second block Saturday afternoon and not only stayed there through the tourney, but increased his Petersen Point lead with every four-game series.

He averaged 216, plus, for the 40 games to nab the city match-game title with 202.11 Petersen Points, and he, along with Dan Toronski, Allie Clarke, Joe Hovancsek, Jack Vojticek and Frank Halek will compete in the BPAA National All-Star Tournament in Kansas City, Mo., next January.

"I never think about bowling while I wait for my turn to bowl," Thompson asserted, "instead, I concentrate on music. Any and all kinds of music.

"The only time I concentrate on my bowling is when I pick up my ball, look at the pins and throw the ball down the lane.

"Then I start thinking of music again."

Thompson recently read a book on self-hypnosis *(How You Can Bowl Better Using Self-Hypnosis)* which is supposed to help keglers.

"I'll tell you one thing," 24-year old Thompson commented, "it helped me and it helped me plenty.

"Self-hypnosis helps me relax. I am no longer tense or nervous. I am at ease and feel peaceful all over."

It may be the hypnosis or it may be the music he hears, but, in this reporter's opinion, what makes Al Thompson a superb bowler today is his delivery, his determination, his attitude, his will to win and his desire to be the best bowler in the nation.

Which, some day, he just might be.

Thompson fires the ball with a smooth follow through and when the ball leaves his hand, it travels with authority.

He throws a strong ball, one which holds the line he has selected for it. And when it hits the pins, it smashes them with a resounding crack.

The pins know that they were hit.

And so do the spectators.

Thompson works hard on every shot, whether he is aiming at all ten sticks, or whether he is attempting to convert a spare or a spilt.

He wants every pin he can get and nothing will stop him from getting them.

"Bowling is my livelihood," he says, "and I want to be the best."

In capturing the match-game crown, Thompson racked up four-game totals of 838-927-909-826-921-867-949, including a 270 game, 814 and 864.

Only in the final round, the knockdown, did he take it easy. He shot only 746.

Al Thompson has come a long way in bowling in just one year.

And, in our opinion, he will go further.

He is an excellent bowler now and will become even better.

Q: I have heard there is a record that hypnotizes you and gives you posthypnotic suggestions to improve your bowling game. Can this be effective?

A: Yes, Professor Richard Carl Spurney, well-known psychologist, with a staff of bowling experts including Bud Hodgson, George Malhiot, Don Harrison, and Howard Holmes has made such a record. It can be extremely effective in improving your bowling game and adding to your confidence. This 33⅓ rpm record is called BOWL-A-STRIKE. It sells for $5 and can be obtained where you bowl or directly from the Wilshire Book Company, 12015 Sherman Road, North Hollywood, California 91605.

Q: Where can I get help should I have further questions or difficulties in using self-hypnosis to improve my game?

A: Read the next chapter. It was meant just for you.

Chapter 14

Your Free Bowling League

Welcome to the fraternity of those who have attained the upper level in bowling thinking! If you have accepted the proof that self-hypnosis is the secret of consistent and better bowling, you are on your way to a higher average.

Should you have any questions, doubts or difficulties in using self-hypnosis to improve your game, please write to:

> Bowling League
> Wilshire Book Company
> 12015 Sherman Road
> North Hollywood, California 91605

Your letter will be answered promptly. Please enclose a self-addressed, stamped envelope.

After you have used self-hypnosis and have experienced the subconscious feel, you will become as enthusiastic as many of the bowlers who have discovered it. Many write the Bowling League telling of their experiences and ideas concerning its application to bowling.

A PERSONAL WORD FROM MELVIN POWERS
PUBLISHER, WILSHIRE BOOK COMPANY

Dear Friend:

My goal is to publish interesting, informative, and inspirational books. You can help me accomplish this by answering the following questions, either by phone or by mail. Or, if convenient for you, I would welcome the opportunity to visit with you in my office and hear your comments in person.

Did you enjoy reading this book? Why?

Would you enjoy reading another similar book?

What idea in the book impressed you the most?

If applicable to your situation, have you incorporated this idea in your daily life?

Is there a chapter that could serve as a theme for an entire book? Please explain.

If you have an idea for a book, I would welcome discussing it with you. If you already have one in progress, write or call me concerning possible publcation. I can be reached at (213) 875-1711 or (213) 983-1105.

Sincerely yours,

MELVIN POWERS

12015 Sherman Road
North Hollywood, California 91605

MELVIN POWERS SELF-IMPROVEMENT LIBRARY

ASTROLOGY

ASTROLOGY: A FASCINATING HISTORY *P. Naylor*	2.00
ASTROLOGY: HOW TO CHART YOUR HOROSCOPE *Max Heindel*	3.00
ASTROLOGY: YOUR PERSONAL SUN-SIGN GUIDE *Beatrice Ryder*	3.00
ASTROLOGY FOR EVERYDAY LIVING *Janet Harris*	2.00
ASTROLOGY MADE EASY *Astarte*	3.00
ASTROLOGY MADE PRACTICAL *Alexandra Kayhle*	3.00
ASTROLOGY, ROMANCE, YOU AND THE STARS *Anthony Norvell*	4.00
MY WORLD OF ASTROLOGY *Sydney Omarr*	4.00
THOUGHT DIAL *Sydney Omarr*	3.00
ZODIAC REVEALED *Rupert Gleadow*	2.00

BRIDGE

BRIDGE BIDDING MADE EASY *Edwin B. Kantar*	5.00
BRIDGE CONVENTIONS *Edwin B. Kantar*	4.00
BRIDGE HUMOR *Edwin B. Kantar*	3.00
COMPETITIVE BIDDING IN MODERN BRIDGE *Edgar Kaplan*	4.00
DEFENSIVE BRIDGE PLAY COMPLETE *Edwin B. Kantar*	10.00
HOW TO IMPROVE YOUR BRIDGE *Alfred Sheinwold*	2.00
INTRODUCTION TO DEFENDER'S PLAY *Edwin B. Kantar*	3.00
SHORT CUT TO WINNING BRIDGE *Alfred Sheinwold*	3.00
TEST YOUR BRIDGE PLAY *Edwin B. Kantar*	3.00
WINNING DECLARER PLAY *Dorothy Hayden Truscott*	4.00

BUSINESS, STUDY & REFERENCE

CONVERSATION MADE EASY *Elliot Russell*	2.00
EXAM SECRET *Dennis B. Jackson*	2.00
FIX-IT BOOK *Arthur Symons*	2.00
HOW TO DEVELOP A BETTER SPEAKING VOICE *M. Hellier*	2.00
HOW TO MAKE A FORTUNE IN REAL ESTATE *Albert Winnikoff*	3.00
INCREASE YOUR LEARNING POWER *Geoffrey A. Dudley*	2.00
MAGIC OF NUMBERS *Robert Tocquet*	2.00
PRACTICAL GUIDE TO BETTER CONCENTRATION *Melvin Powers*	2.00
PRACTICAL GUIDE TO PUBLIC SPEAKING *Maurice Forley*	3.00
7 DAYS TO FASTER READING *William S. Schaill*	3.00
SONGWRITERS RHYMING DICTIONARY *Jane Shaw Whitfield*	5.00
SPELLING MADE EASY *Lester D. Basch & Dr. Milton Finkelstein*	2.00
STUDENT'S GUIDE TO BETTER GRADES *J. A. Rickard*	2.00
TEST YOURSELF—Find Your Hidden Talent *Jack Shafer*	2.00
YOUR WILL & WHAT TO DO ABOUT IT *Attorney Samuel G. Kling*	3.00

CALLIGRAPHY

CALLIGRAPHY—The Art of Beautfiul Writing *Katherine Jeffares*	5.00

CHESS & CHECKERS

BEGINNER'S GUIDE TO WINNING CHESS *Fred Reinfeld*	3.00
BETTER CHESS—How to Play *Fred Reinfeld*	2.00
CHECKERS MADE EASY *Tom Wiswell*	2.00
CHESS IN TEN EASY LESSONS *Larry Evans*	3.00
CHESS MADE EASY *Milton L. Hanauer*	3.00
CHESS MASTERY—A New Approach *Fred Reinfeld*	2.00
CHESS PROBLEMS FOR BEGINNERS *edited by Fred Reinfeld*	2.00
CHESS SECRETS REVEALED *Fred Reinfeld*	2.00
CHESS STRATEGY—An Expert's Guide *Fred Reinfeld*	2.00
CHESS TACTICS FOR BEGINNERS *edited by Fred Reinfeld*	2.00
CHESS THEORY & PRACTICE *Morry & Mitchell*	2.00
HOW TO WIN AT CHECKERS *Fred Reinfeld*	2.00
1001 BRILLIANT WAYS TO CHECKMATE *Fred Reinfeld*	3.00
1001 WINNING CHESS SACRIFICES & COMBINATIONS *Fred Reinfeld*	3.00
SOVIET CHESS *Edited by R. G. Wade*	3.00

COOKERY & HERBS

CULPEPER'S HERBAL REMEDIES *Dr. Nicholas Culpeper*	2.00
FAST GOURMET COOKBOOK *Poppy Cannon*	2.50

_____ MAKING MONEY AT THE RACES *David Barr*		3.00
_____ PAYDAY AT THE RACES *Les Conklin*		2.00
_____ SMART HANDICAPPING MADE EASY *William Bauman*		3.00
_____ SUCCESS AT THE HARNESS RACES *Barry Meadow*		2.50
_____ WINNING AT THE HARNESS RACES—An Expert's Guide *Nick Cammarano*		3.00

HUMOR

_____ HOW TO BE A COMEDIAN FOR FUN & PROFIT *King & Laufer*	2.00
_____ JOKE TELLER'S HANDBOOK *Bob Orben*	3.00

HYPNOTISM

_____ ADVANCED TECHNIQUES OF HYPNOSIS *Melvin Powers*	2.00
_____ BRAINWASHING AND THE CULTS *Paul A. Verdier, Ph.D.*	3.00
_____ CHILDBIRTH WITH HYPNOSIS *William S. Kroger, M.D.*	3.00
_____ HOW TO SOLVE Your Sex Problems with Self-Hypnosis *Frank S. Caprio, M.D.*	3.00
_____ HOW TO STOP SMOKING THRU SELF-HYPNOSIS *Leslie M. LeCron*	3.00
_____ HOW TO USE AUTO-SUGGESTION EFFECTIVELY *John Duckworth*	3.00
_____ HOW YOU CAN BOWL BETTER USING SELF-HYPNOSIS *Jack Heise*	3.00
_____ HOW YOU CAN PLAY BETTER GOLF USING SELF-HYPNOSIS *Jack Heise*	2.00
_____ HYPNOSIS AND SELF-HYPNOSIS *Bernard Hollander, M.D.*	3.00
_____ HYPNOTISM *(Originally published in 1893)* *Carl Sextus*	3.00
_____ HYPNOTISM & PSYCHIC PHENOMENA *Simeon Edmunds*	3.00
_____ HYPNOTISM MADE EASY *Dr. Ralph Winn*	3.00
_____ HYPNOTISM MADE PRACTICAL *Louis Orton*	3.00
_____ HYPNOTISM REVEALED *Melvin Powers*	2.00
_____ HYPNOTISM TODAY *Leslie LeCron and Jean Bordeaux, Ph.D.*	4.00
_____ MODERN HYPNOSIS *Lesley Kuhn & Salvatore Russo, Ph.D.*	4.00
_____ NEW CONCEPTS OF HYPNOSIS *Bernard C. Gindes, M.D.*	4.00
_____ NEW SELF-HYPNOSIS *Paul Adams*	3.00
_____ POST-HYPNOTIC INSTRUCTIONS—Suggestions for Therapy *Arnold Furst*	3.00
_____ PRACTICAL GUIDE TO SELF-HYPNOSIS *Melvin Powers*	2.00
_____ PRACTICAL HYPNOTISM *Philip Magonet, M.D.*	2.00
_____ SECRETS OF HYPNOTISM *S. J. Van Pelt, M.D.*	3.00
_____ SELF-HYPNOSIS Its Theory, Technique & Application *Melvin Powers*	2.00
_____ SELF-HYPNOSIS A Conditioned-Response Technique *Laurance Sparks*	4.00
_____ THERAPY THROUGH HYPNOSIS *edited by Raphael H. Rhodes*	3.00

JUDAICA

_____ HOW TO LIVE A RICHER & FULLER LIFE *Rabbi Edgar F. Magnin*	2.00
_____ MODERN ISRAEL *Lily Edelman*	2.00
_____ ROMANCE OF HASSIDISM *Jacob S. Minkin*	2.50
_____ SERVICE OF THE HEART *Evelyn Garfiel, Ph.D.*	4.00
_____ STORY OF ISRAEL IN COINS *Jean & Maurice Gould*	2.00
_____ STORY OF ISRAEL IN STAMPS *Maxim & Gabriel Shamir*	1.00
_____ TONGUE OF THE PROPHETS *Robert St. John*	3.00
_____ TREASURY OF COMFORT *edited by Rabbi Sidney Greenberg*	4.00

JUST FOR WOMEN

_____ COSMOPOLITAN'S GUIDE TO MARVELOUS MEN Fwd. by *Helen Gurley Brown*	3.00
_____ COSMOPOLITAN'S HANG-UP HANDBOOK Foreword by *Helen Gurley Brown*	4.00
_____ COSMOPOLITAN'S LOVE BOOK—A Guide to Ecstasy in Bed	3.00
_____ COSMOPOLITAN'S NEW ETIQUETTE GUIDE Fwd. by *Helen Gurley Brown*	4.00
_____ I AM A COMPLEAT WOMEN *Doris Hagopian & Karen O'Connor Sweeney*	3.00
_____ JUST FOR WOMEN—A Guide to the Female Body *Richard E. Sand, M.D.*	4.00
_____ NEW APPROACHES TO SEX IN MARRIAGE *John E. Eichenlaub, M.D.*	3.00
_____ SEXUALLY ADEQUATE FEMALE *Frank S. Caprio, M.D.*	2.00
_____ YOUR FIRST YEAR OF MARRIAGE *Dr. Tom McGinnis*	3.00

MARRIAGE, SEX & PARENTHOOD

_____ ABILITY TO LOVE *Dr. Allan Fromme*	5.00
_____ ENCYCLOPEDIA OF MODERN SEX & LOVE TECHNIQUES *Macandrew*	4.00
_____ GUIDE TO SUCCESSFUL MARRIAGE *Drs. Albert Ellis & Robert Harper*	3.00
_____ HOW TO RAISE AN EMOTIONALLY HEALTHY, HAPPY CHILD *A. Ellis*	3.00
_____ IMPOTENCE & FRIGIDITY *Edwin W. Hirsch, M.D.*	3.00
_____ SEX WITHOUT GUILT *Albert Ellis, Ph.D.*	3.00

SEXUALLY ADEQUATE MALE *Frank S. Caprio, M.D.*		3.00

METAPHYSICS & OCCULT

BOOK OF TALISMANS, AMULETS & ZODIACAL GEMS *William Pavitt*	4.00
CONCENTRATION—A Guide to Mental Mastery *Mouni Sadhu*	3.00
CRITIQUES OF GOD *Edited by Peter Angeles*	7.00
DREAMS & OMENS REVEALED *Fred Gettings*	2.00
EXTRASENSORY PERCEPTION *Simeon Edmunds*	2.00
EXTRA-TERRESTRIAL INTELLIGENCE—The First Encounter	6.00
FORTUNE TELLING WITH CARDS *P. Foli*	2.00
HANDWRITING ANALYSIS MADE EASY *John Marley*	2.00
HANDWRITING TELLS *Nadya Olyanova*	5.00
HOW TO UNDERSTAND YOUR DREAMS *Geoffrey A. Dudley*	2.00
ILLUSTRATED YOGA *William Zorn*	3.00
IN DAYS OF GREAT PEACE *Mouni Sadhu*	3.00
KING SOLOMON'S TEMPLE IN THE MASONIC TRADITION *Alex Horne*	5.00
LSD—THE AGE OF MIND *Bernard Roseman*	2.00
MAGICIAN—His training and work *W. E. Butler*	2.00
MEDITATION *Mouni Sadhu*	4.00
MODERN NUMEROLOGY *Morris C. Goodman*	3.00
NUMEROLOGY—ITS FACTS AND SECRETS *Ariel Yvon Taylor*	2.00
PALMISTRY MADE EASY *Fred Gettings*	3.00
PALMISTRY MADE PRACTICAL *Elizabeth Daniels Squire*	3.00
PALMISTRY SECRETS REVEALED *Henry Frith*	2.00
PRACTICAL YOGA *Ernest Wood*	3.00
PROPHECY IN OUR TIME *Martin Ebon*	2.50
PSYCHOLOGY OF HANDWRITING *Nadya Olyanova*	3.00
SEEING INTO THE FUTURE *Harvey Day*	2.00
SUPERSTITION—Are you superstitious? *Eric Maple*	2.00
TAROT *Mouni Sadhu*	5.00
TAROT OF THE BOHEMIANS *Papus*	5.00
TEST YOUR ESP *Martin Ebon*	2.00
WAYS TO SELF-REALIZATION *Mouni Sadhu*	3.00
WHAT YOUR HANDWRITING REVEALS *Albert E. Hughes*	2.00
WITCHCRAFT, MAGIC & OCCULTISM—A Fascinating History *W. B. Crow*	3.00
WITCHCRAFT—THE SIXTH SENSE *Justine Glass*	2.00
WORLD OF PSYCHIC RESEARCH *Hereward Carrington*	2.00
YOU CAN ANALYZE HANDWRITING *Robert Holder*	2.00

SELF-HELP & INSPIRATIONAL

CYBERNETICS WITHIN US *Y. Saparina*	3.00
DAILY POWER FOR JOYFUL LIVING *Dr. Donald Curtis*	3.00
DOCTOR PSYCHO-CYBERNETICS *Maxwell Maltz, M.D.*	3.00
DYNAMIC THINKING *Melvin Powers*	2.00
EXUBERANCE—Your Guide to Happiness & Fulfillment *Dr. Paul Kurtz*	3.00
GREATEST POWER IN THE UNIVERSE *U. S. Andersen*	4.00
GROW RICH WHILE YOU SLEEP *Ben Sweetland*	3.00
GROWTH THROUGH REASON *Albert Ellis, Ph.D.*	4.00
GUIDE TO DEVELOPING YOUR POTENTIAL *Herbert A. Otto, Ph.D.*	3.00
GUIDE TO LIVING IN BALANCE *Frank S. Caprio, M.D.*	2.00
HELPING YOURSELF WITH APPLIED PSYCHOLOGY *R. Henderson*	2.00
HELPING YOURSELF WITH PSYCHIATRY *Frank S. Caprio, M.D.*	2.00
HOW TO ATTRACT GOOD LUCK *A. H. Z. Carr*	3.00
HOW TO CONTROL YOUR DESTINY *Norvell*	3.00
HOW TO DEVELOP A WINNING PERSONALITY *Martin Panzer*	3.00
HOW TO DEVELOP AN EXCEPTIONAL MEMORY *Young & Gibson*	4.00
HOW TO OVERCOME YOUR FEARS *M. P. Leahy, M.D.*	2.00
HOW YOU CAN HAVE CONFIDENCE AND POWER *Les Giblin*	3.00
HUMAN PROBLEMS & HOW TO SOLVE THEM *Dr. Donald Curtis*	3.00
I CAN *Ben Sweetland*	4.00
I WILL *Ben Sweetland*	3.00
LEFT-HANDED PEOPLE *Michael Barsley*	3.00

_____MAGIC IN YOUR MIND *U. S. Andersen*	4.00
_____MAGIC OF THINKING BIG *Dr. David J. Schwartz*	3.00
_____MAGIC POWER OF YOUR MIND *Walter M. Germain*	4.00
_____MENTAL POWER THROUGH SLEEP SUGGESTION *Melvin Powers*	2.00
_____NEW GUIDE TO RATIONAL LIVING *Albert Ellis, Ph.D. & R. Harper, Ph.D.*	3.00
_____OUR TROUBLED SELVES *Dr. Allan Fromme*	3.00
_____PRACTICAL GUIDE TO SUCCESS & POPULARITY *C. W. Bailey*	2.00
_____PSYCHO-CYBERNETICS *Maxwell Maltz, M.D.*	2.00
_____SCIENCE OF MIND IN DAILY LIVING *Dr. Donald Curtis*	3.00
_____SECRET POWER OF THE PYRAMIDS *U. S. Andersen*	4.00
_____SECRET OF SECRETS *U. S. Andersen*	4.00
_____STUTTERING AND WHAT YOU CAN DO ABOUT IT *W. Johnson, Ph.D.*	2.50
_____SUCCESS-CYBERNETICS *U. S. Andersen*	4.00
_____10 DAYS TO A GREAT NEW LIFE *William E. Edwards*	3.00
_____THINK AND GROW RICH *Napoleon Hill*	3.00
_____THREE MAGIC WORDS *U. S. Andersen*	4.00
_____TREASURY OF THE ART OF LIVING *Sidney S. Greenberg*	5.00
_____YOU ARE NOT THE TARGET *Laura Huxley*	3.00
_____YOUR SUBCONSCIOUS POWER *Charles M. Simmons*	4.00
_____YOUR THOUGHTS CAN CHANGE YOUR LIFE *Dr. Donald Curtis*	3.00

SPORTS

_____ARCHERY—An Expert's Guide *Dan Stamp*	2.00
_____BICYCLING FOR FUN AND GOOD HEALTH *Kenneth E. Luther*	2.00
_____BILLIARDS—Pocket • Carom • Three Cushion *Clive Cottingham, Jr.*	2.00
_____CAMPING-OUT 101 Ideas & Activities *Bruno Knobel*	2.00
_____COMPLETE GUIDE TO FISHING *Vlad Evanoff*	2.00
_____HOW TO WIN AT POCKET BILLIARDS *Edward D. Knuchell*	3.00
_____LEARNING & TEACHING SOCCER SKILLS *Eric Worthington*	3.00
_____MOTORCYCLING FOR BEGINNERS *I. G. Edmonds*	2.00
_____PRACTICAL BOATING *W. S. Kals*	3.00
_____RACQUETBALL MADE EASY *Steve Lubarsky, Rod Delson & Jack Scagnetti*	3.00
_____SECRET OF BOWLING STRIKES *Dawson Taylor*	3.00
_____SECRET OF PERFECT PUTTING *Horton Smith & Dawson Taylor*	3.00
_____SECRET WHY FISH BITE *James Westman*	2.00
_____SOCCER—The game & how to play it *Gary Rosenthal*	2.00
_____STARTING SOCCER *Edward F. Dolan, Jr.*	2.00
_____TABLE TENNIS MADE EASY *Johnny Leach*	2.00

TENNIS LOVERS' LIBRARY

_____BEGINNER'S GUIDE TO WINNING TENNIS *Helen Hull Jacobs*	2.00
_____HOW TO BEAT BETTER TENNIS PLAYERS *Loring Fiske*	4.00
_____HOW TO IMPROVE YOUR TENNIS—Style, Strategy & Analysis *C. Wilson*	2.00
_____INSIDE TENNIS—Techniques of Winning *Jim Leighton*	3.00
_____PLAY TENNIS WITH ROSEWALL *Ken Rosewall*	2.00
_____PSYCH YOURSELF TO BETTER TENNIS *Dr. Walter A. Luszki*	2.00
_____SUCCESSFUL TENNIS *Neale Fraser*	2.00
_____TENNIS FOR BEGINNERS *Dr. H. A. Murray*	2.00
_____TENNIS MADE EASY *Joel Brecheen*	2.00
_____WEEKEND TENNIS—How to have fun & win at the same time *Bill Talbert*	3.00
_____WINNING WITH PERCENTAGE TENNIS—Smart Strategy *Jack Lowe*	2.00

WILSHIRE PET LIBRARY

_____DOG OBEDIENCE TRAINING *Gust Kessopulos*	3.00
_____DOG TRAINING MADE EASY & FUN *John W. Kellogg*	2.00
_____HOW TO BRING UP YOUR PET DOG *Kurt Unkelbach*	2.00
_____HOW TO RAISE & TRAIN YOUR PUPPY *Jeff Griffen*	2.00
_____PIGEONS: HOW TO RAISE & TRAIN THEM *William H. Allen, Jr.*	2.00

WILSHIRE HORSE LOVERS' LIBRARY

_____AMATEUR HORSE BREEDER *A. C. Leighton Hardman*	3.00
_____AMERICAN QUARTER HORSE IN PICTURES *Margaret Cabell Self*	3.00
_____APPALOOSA HORSE *Donna & Bill Richardson*	3.00
_____ARABIAN HORSE *Reginald S. Summerhays*	2.00
_____ART OF WESTERN RIDING *Suzanne Norton Jones*	3.00
_____AT THE HORSE SHOW *Margaret Cabell Self*	3.00
_____BACK-YARD FOAL *Peggy Jett Pittinger*	3.00
_____BACK-YARD HORSE *Peggy Jett Pittinger*	3.00
_____BASIC DRESSAGE *Jean Froissard*	2.00
_____BEGINNER'S GUIDE TO HORSEBACK RIDING *Sheila Wall*	2.00
_____BEGINNER'S GUIDE TO THE WESTERN HORSE *Natlee Kenoyer*	2.00
_____BITS—THEIR HISTORY, USE AND MISUSE *Louis Taylor*	3.00
_____BREAKING & TRAINING THE DRIVING HORSE *Doris Ganton*	2.00
_____BREAKING YOUR HORSE'S BAD HABITS *W. Dayton Sumner*	3.00
_____CAVALRY MANUAL OF HORSEMANSHIP *Gordon Wright*	3.00
_____COMPLETE TRAINING OF HORSE AND RIDER *Colonel Alois Podhajsky*	4.00
_____DISORDERS OF THE HORSE & WHAT TO DO ABOUT THEM *E. Hanauer*	2.00
_____DOG TRAINING MADE EASY & FUN *John W. Kellogg*	2.00
_____DRESSAGE—A Study of the Finer Points in Riding *Henry Wynmalen*	4.00
_____DRIVING HORSES *Sallie Walrond*	2.00
_____ENDURANCE RIDING *Ann Hyland*	2.00
_____EQUITATION *Jean Froissard*	4.00
_____FIRST AID FOR HORSES *Dr. Charles H. Denning, Jr.*	2.00
_____FUN OF RAISING A COLT *Rubye & Frank Griffith*	3.00
_____FUN ON HORSEBACK *Margaret Cabell Self*	4.00
_____GYMKHANA GAMES *Natlee Kenoyer*	2.00
_____HORSE DISEASES—Causes, Symptoms & Treatment *Dr. H. G. Belschner*	3.00
_____HORSE OWNER'S CONCISE GUIDE *Elsie V. Hanauer*	2.00
_____HORSE SELECTION & CARE FOR BEGINNERS *George H. Conn*	3.00
_____HORSE SENSE—A complete guide to riding and care *Alan Deacon*	4.00
_____HORSEBACK RIDING FOR BEGINNERS *Louis Taylor*	4.00
_____HORSEBACK RIDING MADE EASY & FUN *Sue Henderson Coen*	3.00
_____HORSES—Their Selection, Care & Handling *Margaret Cabell Self*	3.00
_____HOW TO BUY A BETTER HORSE & SELL THE HORSE YOU OWN	3.00
_____HOW TO ENJOY YOUR QUARTER HORSE *Williard H. Porter*	3.00
_____HUNTER IN PICTURES *Margaret Cabell Self*	2.00
_____ILLUSTRATED BOOK OF THE HORSE *S. Sidney* (8½" x 11½")	10.00
_____ILLUSTRATED HORSE MANAGEMENT—400 Illustrations *Dr. E. Mayhew*	6.00
_____ILLUSTRATED HORSE TRAINING *Captain M. H. Hayes*	5.00
_____ILLUSTRATED HORSEBACK RIDING FOR BEGINNERS *Jeanne Mellin*	2.00
_____JUMPING—Learning & Teaching *Jean Froissard*	3.00
_____KNOW ALL ABOUT HORSES *Harry Disston*	3.00
_____LAME HORSE—Causes, Symptoms & Treatment *Dr. James R. Rooney*	3.00
_____LAW & YOUR HORSE *Edward H. Greene*	3.00
_____LIPIZZANERS & THE SPANISH RIDING SCHOOL *W. Reuter* (4¼" x 6")	2.50
_____MANUAL OF HORSEMANSHIP *Harold Black*	5.00
_____MORGAN HORSE IN PICTURES *Margaret Cabell Self*	2.00
_____MOVIE HORSES—The Fascinating Techniques of Training *Anthony Amaral*	2.00
_____POLICE HORSES *Judith Campbell*	2.00
_____PRACTICAL GUIDE TO HORSESHOEING	3.00
_____PRACTICAL GUIDE TO OWNING YOUR OWN HORSE *Steven D. Price*	2.00
_____PRACTICAL HORSE PSYCHOLOGY *Moyra Williams*	3.00
_____PROBLEM HORSES Guide for Curing Serious Behavior Habits *Summerhays*	2.00
_____REINSMAN OF THE WEST—BRIDLES & BITS *Ed Connell*	4.00
_____RESCHOOLING THE THOROUGHBRED *Peggy Jett Pittenger*	3.00
_____RIDE WESTERN *Louis Taylor*	3.00
_____SCHOOLING YOUR YOUNG HORSE *George Wheatley*	2.00
_____STABLE MANAGEMENT FOR THE OWNER-GROOM *George Wheatley*	4.00
_____STALLION MANAGEMENT—A Guide for Stud Owners *A. C. Hardman*	3.00
_____TEACHING YOUR HORSE TO JUMP *W. J. Froud*	2.00
_____TRAIL HORSES & TRAIL RIDING *Anne & Perry Westbrook*	2.00
_____TRAINING YOUR HORSE TO SHOW *Neale Haley*	3.00
_____TREATING COMMON DISEASES OF YOUR HORSE *Dr. George H. Conn*	3.00
_____TREATING HORSE AILMENTS *G. W. Serth*	2.00
_____WESTERN HORSEBACK RIDING *Glen Balch*	3.00
_____WONDERFUL WORLD OF PONIES *Peggy Jett Pittenger* (8½" x 11½")	4.00
_____YOU AND YOUR PONY *Pepper Mainwaring Healey* (8½" x 11")	6.00
_____YOUR FIRST HORSE *George C. Saunders, M.D.*	3.00
_____YOUR PONY BOOK *Hermann Wiederhold*	2.00
_____YOUR WESTERN HORSE *Nelson C. Nye*	2.00

The books listed above can be obtained from your book dealer or directly from Melvin Powers. When ordering, please remit 30¢ per book postage & handling. Send for our free illustrated catalog of self-improvement books.

Melvin Powers
12015 Sherman Road, No. Hollywood, California 91605

THE SECRET OF BOWLING STRIKES
by Dawson Taylor

Contents:

1. The Squeeze 2. The Equipment for Bowling 3. The Etiquette of Bowling 4. The Scoring Marks in Bowling 5. The Language of Bowling 6. The Scoring in Bowling, or How to Add by 10's 7. The Strategy of Bowling 8. Taking Advantage of the "Angle" 9. The Fundamentals of Bowling 10. The Practical Application of the Fundamentals 11. How to Practice Bowling Away from the Lane 12. The Physiology of Bowling 13. The Second Ball 14. Splits and What to Do About Them 15. Other Variations in Converting Spares 16. How to Throw a Straight Ball 17. Some Common Faults in Bowling 18. Develop Your Own Style 19. What to Do When You Are "In Trouble."   **128 Pages ... $3**

PSYCHO-CYBERNETICS
A New Technique for Using Your Subconscious Power
by Maxwell Maltz, M.D., F.I.C.S.

Contents:

1. The Self Image: Your Key to a Better Life 2. Discovering the Success Mechanism within You 3. Imagination—The First Key to Your Success Mechanism 4. Dehypnotize Yourself from False Beliefs 5. How to Utilize the Power of Rational Thinking 6. Relax and Let Your Success Mechanism Work for You 7. You Can Acquire the Habit of Happiness 8. Ingredients of the Success-Type Personality and How to Acquire Them 9. The Failure Mechanism: How to Make It Work For You Instead of Against You 10. How to Remove Emotional Scars, or How to Give Yourself an Emotional Face Lift 11. How to Unlock Your Real Personality 12. Do-It-Yourself Tranquilizers That Bring Peace of Mind 13. How to Turn a Crisis into a Creative Opportunity 14. How to Get "That Winning Feeling" 15. More Years of Life—More Life in Your Years. **268 Pages ... $2**

PRACTICAL GUIDE TO BETTER CONCENTRATION
by Melvin Powers & Robert S. Starrett

Contents:

1. What You Should Know About Concentration 2. The Anatomy of Concentration 3. Psychological Factors in Concentration 4. Use Your Subconscious for Better Concentration 5. The Technique for Developing Your Powers of Concentration 6. Special Techniques for Better Concentration, Reading and Learning 7. Concentration and Group Learning 8. Communication and Semantics 9. Juvenile Delinquency, Crime and Learning 10. Tests and Examinations 11. Questions and Answers 12. Your Free Concentration Service.   **130 Pages ... $2**

A PRACTICAL GUIDE TO SELF-HYPNOSIS
by Melvin Powers

Contents:

1. What You Should Know About Self-Hypnosis 2. What About the Dangers of Hypnosis? 3. Is Hypnosis the Answer? 4. How Does Self-Hypnosis Work? 5. How to Arouse Yourself From the Self-Hypnotic State 6. How to Attain Self-Hypnosis 7. Deepening the Self-Hypnotic State 8. What You Should Know About Becoming an Excellent Subject 9. Techniques for Reaching the Somnambulistic State 10. A New Approach to Self-Hypnosis When All Else Fails 11. Psychological Aids and Their Function 12. The Nature of Hypnosis 13. Practical Applications of Self-Hypnosis.   **120 Pages ... $2**

THE MAGIC OF THINKING BIG
by David J. Schwartz, Ph.D.

Contents:

1. Believe You Can Succeed and You Will 2. Cure Yourself of Excusitis, the Failure Disease 3. Build Confidence and Destroy Fear 4. How to Think Big 5. How to Think and Dream Creatively 6. You Are What You Think You Are 7. Manage Your Environment: Go First Class 8. Make Your Attitudes Your Allies 9. Think Right Towards People 10. Get the Action Habit 11. How to Turn Defeat Into Victory 12. Use Goals to Help You Grow 13. How to Think Like a Leader.   **225 Pages ... $3**

NOTES

NOTES

NOTES

NOTES

NOTES